TRUE WEST

ARTS, TRADITIONS, AND CELEBRATIONS

By Christine Mather

Photographs by Jack Parsons
Design by Paul Hardy

CLARKSON POTTER/PUBLISHERS
NEW YORK

To my parents, Chris and Genne Regas. They first took me to live in the West and much later followed me west—no matter where I have roamed they have always been with me.

◆━◆━◆

It won't be a century before the West is simply the true America with thought, type and life of its own kind.

Owen Wister, July 10, 1885

Text copyright © 1992 by Christine Mather
Photographs copyright © 1992 by Jack Parsons

Published by Clarkson N. Potter, Inc., 201 East 50th Street, New York, New York 10022. Member of the Crown Publishing Group.
CLARKSON N. POTTER, POTTER and colophon are trademarks of Clarkson N. Potter, Inc.
Manufactured in Japan

Library of Congress Cataloging-in-Publication Data

Mather, Christine.
  True West/by Christine Mather: photographs by Jack Parsons. —1st ed.
    p. cm.
  Includes index.
  1. West (U.S.)—Description and travel—1981—Views. 2. West (U.S.)—Social life and customs. I. Title.
F595.3.M38 1992
978—dc20   91-34493
                                     CIP
ISBN 0-517-58336-4
10 9 8 7 6 5 4 3 2 1
First Edition

CONTENTS

PREFACE

My home is situated less than a mile from the Santa Fe Trail and sits upon land once part of the Sebastian Land Grant, given to a worthy colonist by the king of Spain and much later purchased by Ernest Thompson Seton, the founder of the Boy Scouts of America. Down the road the well-hidden remains of a prehistoric village now called Arroyo Hondo lie on my daily route into Santa Fe. I was not born in the West, but, having lived in Santa Fe for most of my adult life—raising my children, studying its history and art along with my husband, Davis—I have come to love the daily experience of being vividly alive that the West means to me. Our lives here have been influenced and touched by people and places in Oregon, Arizona, and New Mexico, and the spaces we traveled in between. There was Ferona Konopak, who regaled us with tales of life as a Harvey Girl, while generously pouring the scotch; and Pat and Dot Pattison, who seemed to know every well and water right in New Mexico; and Boris, who attempted to enlist my husband in a half-fanciful plan to blow up the Hilton back in the days when Santa Fe development was in its infancy. These folks are gone now but the way they lived has had its influence upon us and others. We have watched double rainbows over Kitchen Mesa at Ghost Ranch; pulled the cactus thorns out of the noses of the dogs; got lost, happily, in the Lukachukai Mountains; and been awed by the lightning hitting the Ponderosa pine. I am not sure who one thanks for such experiences, but each has contributed to the making of this book.

In my hometown there are many who deserve thanks for their efforts on my behalf and their generous spirits: Art Olivas and Dick Rudisill at Photo Archives; the folks at the Museum of International Folk Art; Liddy Miller at Ghost Ranch; Mary Hunt Kahlenberg, Jeff Kask, Mariel Webb, Marie Romero Cash, Emilio and Senaida Romero, Al Luckett, Maurice Dixon, Jim and Elizabeth McGorty, Roger Miller, Chris O'Connell, Jack Pressler, Mike Rodriguez, Tracy Seidman, Luis Tapia, Stoney Wellman, Teresa Archuleta Sagel, and Greg Flores—all are folks who have been great help and company.

In Arizona, Jinx and Spencer Giffords put me up once again and are always there for me. Other terrific Arizonans who aided in this book were the kind people at the Arizona Historical Society and the Fiesta de los Vaqueros in Tucson as well as Ed Mell, Michael Collier, Anne Coe, Tom Paul Schneider, Lloyd Davis, Audrey and Tom Ives, Gretchen Freeman, and Alan Silverman.

For sheer beauty, friendliness, and fun, Wyoming was a revelation. Thanks to Bill and Barbara Schenck, Robin Weiss, and the Donnans and to all those others who made the experience a memorable one: Scott Albrecht at the Crescent H Ranch, Betty and Whit Clayton, and Art Anderson.

Liz Dear and Paul Zarzyski helped shrink the spaces and open doors throughout Montana. Many thanks to Jeff Sailors, Jerry Valdez, and the people at the Montana Historical Society.

We kept going back to Texas for more; it is a treasure, and so too are the many wonderful friends who helped us out. In San Antonio and environs Rowena and David Dillon, Tom Messer and Fred Pottinger, Robert Oliver, and Michael Earny did everything and then some for us. Through their kindnesses we were able to enjoy Mr. and Mrs. Waymon Buchanan, Mr. and Mrs. Charles Nash, the Winedale Historical Center, the LBJ National Historical Park, and the home of Tim and Carol Bolton. Our thanks to Teresa and Tyler Beard, who, in the spirit of Texas, kept opening doors for us so that we were able to meet with Dan and Judy Coates, see the Dixie Dude Ranch, and the R. E. Donaho Saddle Shop, Joe Gish's Old West Museum, the Hatatorium Hat Shop, Eddie Kimmel, and the Stanley Boot Shop. In the Panhandle, Bob Moorehouse, the manager of the Pitchfork Ranch and a fine photographer, couldn't have been more generous; to him and the cowboys of the Pitchfork, our sincere thanks. Down the road at the 6666 Ranch, J. J. Gibson and his family and those who work that fabulous spread are to be thanked for their help. The Ranching Heritage Center in Lubbock was most welcoming; with the great professionals Alvin Davis, Gary Edison, and David Dean, and the support of Texas Tech University, the preservation of a rich heritage seems assured.

Back East, warmest thanks to Deborah Geltman, a fine literary agent, and Paul Hardy, a superb designer. Their help and the continued support and friendship of Lauren Shakely, the outstanding editor of this project, made this publication possible. Thanks to Alberto Vitale our paths were able to cross with Mrs. Louis L'Amour, whose enthusiasm and openness was a great reward. Thanks to Amy Boorstein, Joan Denman, Howard Klein, and Renato Stanisic at Clarkson Potter.

On the home front, my sincere thanks to my fine colleague Jack Parsons, whose wonderful photographs and unwavering friendship carried this book forward, and to his dear wife, Becky, who helps us both. Thanks are due to Melanie West and Alexis Avery, true Westerners, who not only provided research for this book but also joined in the spirit of our family. Amanda and Thais were able to travel with us on a number of occasions; they brought great energy and loads of good memories. My thanks to Davis, the most supportive and caring of partners and love of my life.

Christine Mather
Santa Fe, New Mexico

INTRODUCTION

There is no little irony in entitling a book, magazine, or play "True West." For one thing, there is almost no escaping the myths that have pervaded Western culture: the "truth" about this American phenomenon is that its legend, with all of its bombast and overstatement, is as much a part of its reality as are the humdrum details of everyday life. The True West is a place full of itself, filled with people who love to brag and are convinced that there is plenty to give them pride. For those who live in the West, it can also be too big, too lonely, too demanding—it has never been easy. In the early years, being a Westerner demanded great physical tamina and grit. The efforts of these forerunners left their stamp on the character of the people of the West, making them stoical and determined. Like the often-mentioned informality of the West, these attitudes and behaviors seem bred

Jennie Avery's group toured the West in 1915, taking in the giant redwoods.

in the bone of many Westerners and act like a magnet for others around the world.

The entire experience of the West relates to its grand dimensions. No matter how efficient the highway or comfortable the car, it takes forever to get from one place to another. Journeys now measured in days on the highway were, not so very long ago, counted in months. To the early traders who plied the road from Mexico City to Santa Fe, the journey into the American West was the task of a lifetime, taking a year to go down and back, and then starting all over again. The vast emptiness of the landscape is not just an obstacle, it is the primary attraction of the West. With the opening of the lands beyond the Mississippi, Americans changed forever their concept of themselves.

Facing the challenge of its unexplored territory, America undertook the task in stages, both mentally and physically. Thomas Jefferson gazed toward the unexplored West from his hilltop in Virginia, at a time when Kentucky was considered the edge of the world. The Western Reserve of Massachusetts, what is now Ohio, quickly turned into the Middle West as manifest destiny was fulfilled. The real West finally settled itself as the place that began with the Great Plains and stretched almost to the Pacific Coast. To this day most true Westerners regard the Far, or coastal, West as another world, and California's offbeat reputation continues to confirm this belief. The everchanging frontier has often left doubt about the West's boundaries; a favorite definition is that if you are facing north, the West is to your left.

Before the arrival of Europeans the West was inhabited by peoples whose cultures had been established for millenniums. First among the histories of the West was that of

Young children show their pride in their new frame school in Fargo in 1878, *left.* **Photographer Dana B. Chase shows a chuck wagon used as a serving table in 1890s New Mexico,** *opposite.*

The main street of the mining town of Telluride, Colorado, in 1907 gives the appearance of being built overnight.

Native Americans, who dominated and controlled settlement in the West into the 19th century. Overwhelmed in the East, Native Americans became prime movers in the West, and they continue to own large and important lands, maintain and expand their traditional arts, and follow their religions. Without Navajo blankets, silver jewelry, Pueblo pottery, or countless other crafts and designs, the West would not look Western. Their contributions to the legacy and lore of the West are crucial to all aspects of Western life.

There are two colonial Americas, the one that fills our early history education with the events and people of Plymouth, Jamestown, and Philadelphia, and an earlier less well known colonial America that began with Columbus, continued with Hernán Cortés's entrance into Mexico City, and carries on today in the Hispanic traditions of the Southwest.

For the Spanish, the West was not the west but the north. It was every bit as formidable a frontier for them as it was for the Americans who followed centuries later. Though settlements were established, mission churches built, and rivers and mountains named, the Spanish never gained control of the region. Its bigness overwhelmed them and they literally lived on the edge of survival. Far from the centers of New Spain, the colonists of the northern territories felt as if they were

adrift, and the centers of power and influence did little to assuage their fears. Unable to populate these northern reaches on their own, many Spanish colonists were pleased with the arrival in the mid- to late 19th century of the boisterous, aggressive newcomers from the East who poured into the regions of California, Texas, Arizona, and New Mexico. Those first explorers, adventurers, and merchants from Anglo-America often as not found themselves adapting to and adopting the ways of those who had preceded them. The contributions of the Spanish to the language, lore, and history of the West are immense. By the time the West was officially opened to other Americans via the Santa Fe Trail in the 1820s, many of the patterns and life-style issues of Western life had long been established through the centuries of interaction between Native Americans and Spanish Americans.

The desire to capture this ephemeral scene became a personal goal for a few; the fledgling art of photography, which had emerged from the studio to record the Civil War, found its most fertile ground in the American West. Photography and painting not only revealed the spectacular geography of the West but also its people.

But when the dust settled on this new part of the country, the figure who emerged as America's cultural hero was the cowboy. This character of legend has had an influence far greater than his real existence—there were only a few hundred cowboys in the heyday of the cattle drives, which lasted a few short decades between the Civil War and the turn of the century, before the railroads made the trail ride obsolete. The American cowboy is a figure intimately

Ouray, the chief of the Utes, sat for this photograph by William G. Chamberlain in 1868.

associated with the West, since his very nature seems to summarize what the West represented. His desire for independence and willingness to live on the very edge of civilization, along with his ability, resilience, and enterprise, were all part of the Western experience. The physical demands of his job had a direct appeal to an America that took pride in its agrarian roots and prized those willing to challenge authority—and even civilization—in order to ensure their freedom.

Much of the appeal of the cowboy as we know him today was also a matter of calculated commercialism. Starting with the Wild West shows and leading up to the automobile, alcohol, and cigarette advertisements of our own era, the cowboy has been a convenient symbol of American masculinity. But regardless of the uses and abuses of this quintessentially American creation, the cowboy is nevertheless an appropriate symbol of the True West.

Having left their homes far behind, the explorers, cowboys, and pioneers who settled the West had the opportunity to make their own history as they went along, and they created a set of values that came to define the American character. These new Americans were ambitious but contradictory. They loved the land and found joy in the wilderness, but they also actively squandered the very resources they loved. The new settlers considered Native Americans "noble savages," while at the same time driving them off their native lands or, worse, committing genocide. Nor were Hispanics exempt from their efforts. The 19th-century settlers admired and appropriated Hispanic institutions and customs while laying claim to their lands. This was all part of the "westering" experience for the young nation—an ability to cherish opposing beliefs and to push on despite the effect on those being displaced.

The contradictions appeared also as both a desire for simple utility and a quest for glory. There were elegant opera houses in mining towns and elaborate engravings on spurs. Those who came to settle the West wanted civilization at the same time as they gloried in the lack of it. When the railroad arrived, bringing connections and goods, Westerners embraced these benefits while condemning the trains as iron monsters that tore up the landscape and forced out those in their path.

All ventures in the West seemed to reflect these conflicting sentiments, especially prominent in the ongoing debate over use of limited resources. Recognition of the fragility of what once seemed so infinite has come slowly, at the expense of the integrity of this treasure. When people set out westward in wagon trains with the first manufactured goods, their wagon wheels rolled over the Ogallala aquifer, a vast water reserve millions of years in the making which may run dry in our lifetime. Highways now parallel the ruts those wagon wheels wore in the Plains.

The pioneers, frontier people and explorers of the past lived in a world of daily confrontation—a physically demanding world that required the best of their energies. In their eagerness to survive in the West, they overcame the old adage and their own mortality by taking parts of it with them. Nature's generosity would not be repeated, and the future would demand harder choices and offer fewer alternatives. No longer a place cut off, a place of infinite possibilities, the West has come of age and has recognized its limitations while still reveling in its wide open spaces. The trees that blanket the mountains, the water that flows across state lines, the wary animals that have retreated to the least peopled areas must be accounted for, not plundered. The romance of the West lies not just in its reckless past but in its conservation-minded future. The promise of the West is a new beginning, a hope for the future. Insofar as the West has fulfilled its earlier promise, the debt must now be paid—a debt of recognition for what the West has given our national character, and what we must do to preserve its treasures.

Canuto R. Gonzalez, Jr., relaxed on horseback in New Mexico in the 1930s.

PART ONE

HISPANIC HERITAGE

THE SPANISH SETTLE THE WEST

Although the American West seems younger, both geologically and historically, than the rest of the country, it is in fact more venerable. Here many of the earliest explorers, soldiers, colonists, and priests first came. Long before Jamestown but not too long after Columbus, Francisco Vázquez de Coronado wandered into what is now New Mexico, Arizona, Texas, Oklahoma, and on into Kansas, seeking El Dorado and finding instead Zuni and the Grand Canyon, the Rio Grande and the Llano Estacado. Like his newly enriched cousin, Hernán Cortés, Coronado was hoping to strike it rich in the New World, finding cities of gold like Mexico City. The New World did in fact offer more gold; it simply was not in Kansas.

19

Late 19th-century New Mexican craftsmen framed inexpensive chromolithographic prints with handsome tinwork.

When Columbus returned to Hispaniola, and Cortés docked in Vera Cruz, and later when Coronado marched off into the trackless reaches, they did so with men and horses and firearms and sometimes with cattle and other stock. Sheep, cattle, horses, and Hispanic men and women populated the West over the course of centuries. Not long after the explorers discovered the new territories, colonists settled Santa Fe, and presidios and missions sprang up in Texas, Arizona, and finally California. Silver poured out of Zacatecas, cattle roamed wild in Texas, and herds of wild horses did the same out on the Plains. Coronado never found his Seven Cities or his gold, but he opened the American West. What is now cowboy country, the Sunbelt, and the border was for centuries the claim of Coronado and his heirs—the Spanish.

When the Spanish came to the New World they brought all their attitudes, knowledge, and institutions. Typical of their colonizing style, they almost immediately began to organize, proselytize, and legalize all whom they encountered. Their enthusiasm for this grand New World was prodigious, but the response to these efforts from the native population was often less than enthusiastic. In the northern territory of the Spanish Empire in the New World, up in the Gran Chichimeca, the tough resistance fighters held out against the changes in their world, but for the most part the indigenous North Americans surrendered much of their way of life. In many areas of the Spanish empire the newly arrived colonists forced out the native populations, or worse yet forced them into specific areas for their eventual subjugation. This practice, called *reducción*, placed native peoples in close proximity with one another, causing the rapid spread of disease.

A significant and persistent goal of the Spanish throughout the New World was to bring Roman Catholicism to the native populations. The Jesuits and the Franciscans, the presidios and the missions, grew hand in hand. Out in the wilderness, fortresslike churches and their accompanying mission complexes went up, came down, and went up again. Spain dispatched religious supplies and numerous missionaries to every corner of the expanding empire. Priests were trained in every religious function from music to architecture, since it would be their task to re-create the complexity of religious doctrine and celebration for those totally unfamiliar with the fundamentals of Christianity. By the first half of the 17th century, missionizing activity had begun in earnest as far north as New Mexico. Halted after the Pueblo Revolt of 1680, missions reappeared during the Reconquest by Don Diego de Vargas more than a decade later.

The missions became far more than centers of religious proselytization: they were contact points where traditions and skills were passed from one culture to another. The skills, along with the limited wealth and resources, of the natives were also put to use within the mission complex. California mission priests were especially successful at training natives to care for large herds of cattle, a source of considerable revenue for the church. In New Mexico, colonial administrators put Pueblo people, already skilled in weaving cotton, to work weaving wool as well. Throughout northern New Mexico, Spanish colonists produced wool blankets with their own distinctive patterns in large quantities.

A Mexican *charro* shows the outstanding rope work that developed among the *vaqueros* of northern Mexico and the costume of the working *vaquero* that so influenced the American cowboy.

The primary challenges that the Spanish faced in the West were finding and using water, regulating land use, and developing natural resources. Little has changed from those days 400 years ago. The Spanish not only were the first to pursue the dream of the West, but they were also the first to discover the reality: the West is huge and the governance of it was far beyond the resources of a far-off, mother country. Their colonies on the northern frontier of New Spain lived, for the most part, on the margin. A brutal winter, a bad harvest, rebellious indigenous people, a failed supply train—such vicissitudes pushed their existence to the edge and sometimes over the edge. Added to this abiding hardship was the persistent and nagging fear that no one—no one in a position of authority—really cared about them and their fate. When the supplies arrived on time, when extra soldiers rode in to fortify the presidios, when the mission church received a special gift, and when Santa Anna arrived at the Alamo to let the Texicans know who owned what, life in the colonies seemed good again. But for the most part, throughout the Spanish and Mexican periods, those who lived "up north" suffered many hardships on their own.

The culture that emerged from this life of isolation and want was often quite extraordinary—a true testament to the sensibilities and strengths of Spanish pioneers. To them must go the credit for the most significant architectural monuments in the West—the churches. With few resources and even less guidance, Spanish and Indian builders erected grand statements about their beliefs that stand today as reminders of their devotion. Though dreamers, they were also eminently practical folk who developed methods and tools for the effective management of cattle and horses in the west. Virtually all aspects of the life of the American cowboy, rancher, and cattleman originated in the practices of the Mexican *vaquero* and the methods of the northern *hacendado* (ha-

Musicians at Santa Fe's Fiesta in the late 1930s reflect the great energy and release that the fiesta always generates.

cienda owner). These were the men who first figured out how to raise large herds effectively and transport them to markets. They trained others to carry on these traditions and in so doing passed on centuries of knowledge to denizens of the new continent.

The transfer of this knowledge came along the large borders between what was rapidly becoming part of America and what had once been part of Spain. This great chunk of land—sometimes called the Southwest, once called Northern New Spain—includes what are today the states of California, Texas, Arizona, and New Mexico. It is a region forever in dispute. Today the dispute no longer lies in where the border should be drawn but rather in how we regard this part of America's history and how we regard our neighbors who are so importantly a part of this history. The early arts supported by the Spanish missions—saint making, tinwork, furniture making, embroidery, and weaving—have been revived in the Southwest today. Recognized by museum curators and collectors alike as fine examples of a unique decorative arts tradition, these Hispanic crafts represent an early American history that is as significant as the contributions of the colonists of the East. The Spanish and Mexican experience in the American West is not just a part of the past or a story of "them against us"—it *is* us.

José Dolores Lopez of Cordova, 1935, influenced a generation of woodcarvers in northern New Mexico.

CACTUS COUNTRY

At home with hostility, sun, and dryness, cactus survive in a seemingly lifeless world. Armed and ready spines protrude along their edges, covering their broad surfaces or spreading like tiny hairs overall. Within a corner of our country that appears barren, cacti thrive in astonishing abundance. Over 140 species have been recorded in the Sonoran desert of Arizona and Mexico. Giant saguaros are the quintessential guardians of the desert, with their humanoid forms and great heights. At their feet (and knees) are pincushions, mammalarias, prickly pears, teddy bears, barrels, and hundreds of other varieties. Cacti bloom annually in brilliant pinks, reds, yellows, and purples—intense colors against a monochromatic backdrop.

Shapes and sizes, colors and spines —there are a remarkable number of varieties of cacti in the Sonoran desert. A collection of cacti, *left,* lines a stairway in a home in Arizona. The array of cacti, *right,* are captured in the wild of the Sonoran desert, where they were first seen by Spanish soldiers more than 400 years ago.

MISSION LIFE

Throughout the Southwest, there are churches, missions, cathedrals, and private chapels that reflect the nature and number of the local worshipers. As the crown and the church worked together to carry religion into the wilderness, it quickly became apparent that New World churches could never duplicate the complexity or the splendor of those in Spain. Mission life concentrated on bringing the bare essentials of doctrine to the new converts, while mission buildings, often constructed of the simplest materials and furnishings, were equally minimal. Much of the success of construction and decoration depended upon the skills of the mission priest, who taught his flock not just church doctrine, but European building and decorating techniques. The result of both the simplification and the use of indigenous labor produced a distinctive regional Spanish colonial style of art and architecture. So while churches in urban, central Mexico might be large, elaborately decorated stone structures with silver, gold, and brocade fittings, those built on the far northern frontier were simple adobe chapels with modest interior decor.

Founded by the famed Father Kino and built during the last decades of the 18th century, Tucson's San Xavier del Bac remains one of the most impressive Spanish colonial monuments in America, with much of its original ornament intact. It continues to serve as the church on the Tohono O'odham Reservation, *left. Above,* **a procession of the faithful celebrates the feast day of a locally important religious figure in a small Hispanic village in northern New Mexico at the turn of the century.**

Missions were meant to be self-sufficient communities that would mirror the larger Spanish world. The padres supervised the raising of sheep and cattle, farming, weaving, and other craft specialties. From blacksmithing and plowing to painting and carving, everything Spanish had to be taught and modified for local needs. For Christian education and worship, the priest needed works of art. Padres might paint scenes from the life of Christ, import paintings and carvings from the cities, commission colonists to create church decorations, or teach indigenous people to draw, paint, carve, and sculpt.

So-called mission chains, such as those in northern Sonora, California, Texas, or New Mexico, are the legacy of the meeting of the cultures and the advent of a new religion into the lives of native people.

The San Juan Capistrano Mission, built on the San Antonio River in the 1730s, is evidence of the Franciscans, who erected countless missions in the San Antonio area, *right*. Once self-sufficient, with gardens and workshops, the San Antonio missions are today run by the National Park Service. Many missions continue to serve as active parish churches.

The Virgin of Guadalupe has been updated with an aura of neon, *below.* The modest Mission San Antonio de Valero, *right,* was founded in 1718 and, like the other mission churches of the San Antonio area, served the population of Coahuiltecans. Ironically, this once-quiet mission played a role in Texas's independence from Mexico and is today known as the Alamo.

SAINT MAKERS

E very saint has his day" is literally true in the Hispanic world. The Roman Catholic calendar is filled with days of celebration for each of the many *santos* (saints). Holy orders venerated their founders and introduced them to their converts, along with the many other early Christian and medieval martyrs. San Francisco de Asís, San Antonio de Padua, Santa Barbara, Santa Rosa de Lima, and San José are among the many saints who were highly venerated throughout the Spanish empire. Churches and chapels were built in their honor and towns and cities were named for them. Newborns routinely received names of the saints especially loved in their family. A saint's image was often central to the family altar, and individuals often owned images of their name saints.

Large *retablos* (altarscreens) bearing the images of saints were constructed and painted within the churches. In addition, sculpture was integrated within the *retablos* or placed in niches. Often artists created *re-*

The Virgin awaits her Niño, *left*, in a *bulto* by Marie Romero Cash. A number of other *bultos* by Romero Cash stand in her living room, *right*, which, like the rest of her house, is dedicated to the making of religious folk art. Marie is a student and lover of all New Mexican religious folk art and works in the style and medium of her ancestors. Annually in July she shares a booth with her parents and siblings at the Spanish Market in Santa Fe.

tablos and carvings in their city workshops, then shipped them to the colonies. When currency was available, the local colonists or converts took on the task, gradually developing regional styles of religious art.

Today in Hispanic communities, the *santos* are still indispensable for daily worship and a sense of well-being. Worshipers attend to the *santos* by providing the proper clothing and other attributes necessary for the various times in the religious calendar. Saints are often called upon to bless the congregation and their activities. Each spring in rural areas San Isidro is taken to the fields to bless them and returned in the fall in appreciation for his aid. In the cities, San Jose helps the carpenters. Every aspect of life is shared with the saints.

In New Mexico, local *santeros* (makers of *santos*), rather than city artisans, provided imagery for the village churches. With the coming of the railroads in the 1880s, regionally produced religious art quickly disappeared as mass-produced goods became more readily available. Soon chromolithographic prints replaced hand-adzed and painted *retablos*; plaster statuary supplanted locally made *bultos* (carved wooden sculpture).

Traditional New Mexican religious folk art from the 19th century, such as the Archangel San Miguel, *far left,* and San Antonio de Padua, *left,* remains *in situ* at the old adobe parish churches that dot the landscape of New Mexico's mountains and valleys. A detail of the central *retablo* at the church in Truchas, New Mexico, *above right,* was made by a local artist in the early 19th century. *Right,* San Antonio de Padua is among the most popular saints.

LUIS TAPIA: SANTA FE SANTERO

Luis Tapia works in a simple studio just off the Camino Real (the Royal Road), in Santa Fe. Like the *santeros* of the 18th and 19th centuries, Luis demands a great deal from himself and, like his *antepasados* (ancestors), he is largely self-taught and remarkably productive. *Retablos, bultos,* paintings on canvas, stone sculpture, furniture—all are art forms that

In his studio in Santa Fe, Luis Tapia makes *bultos* and other New Mexican folk art using many of the techniques of bygone *santeros, right. Below,* he paints a *bulto* of the Christ Child.

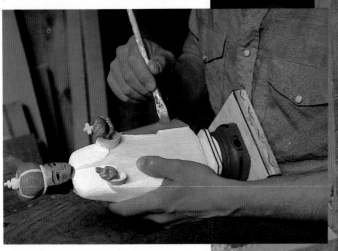

Luis strives to master and improve. Driven to create, he is also part of the preservation movement, assisting in major conservation projects of ancient works. In his own work, he uses traditional methods and materials. For his *santos*, he carves in cottonwood or other local woods, covering them with a fine *yeso* (gesso), and then painting the figures. No matter how much Luis experiments with new formats and different techniques, he has always returned to his roots in Hispanic New Mexican folk art. The results are vibrant examples of religious folk art.

The Lamb of God holding a banner is another carving by Luis Tapia, *below.* The Virgin of Guadalupe, who appeared to the humble Indian Juan Diego, became the most miraculous and significant apparition in the New World, *right.* Her appearance in the hills outside of Mexico City in the 16th century indicated that she had come to serve all the people of the New World. She continues to be the most venerated figure among the Hispanic populations of Latin America.

Like so many colonist and pioneer homes in the West, the house started simply enough. From perhaps one or two rooms the adobe structure kept growing, as the little town of Galisteo, New Mexico, grew. Once the home of fierce Tanos Indians (starved into submission by the late 18th century, and ultimately driven into extinction), Galisteo was a small fortified Spanish town with stone and adobe walls and modest adobe homes. Limited water supply kept Galisteo small.

Humble tin frames filled with the images of the saints were popular among the poor, regional populations of New Mexico and northern Mexico well into the 20th century, *above* and *right.* These frames were made of cast-off tin, scraps of wallpaper or decorative painted paper, and glass. They often had neo-Classic details such as pediments and volutes. *Far right,* a hallway in the Dixon home is filled with the religious art and furnishings of New Mexico and northern Mexico, and includes a number of contemporary *retablos* by *santera* Marie Romero Cash. The bright painted dado and cool white walls are typical of Mexican-style decoration.

The simple dwelling that the scholar and artist Maurice Dixon bought in the 1970s was small and in need of repair. When its adobe weathered from many years exposure to the elements, Dixon patched and refurbished, adding rooms as time and resources permitted. Long a student and aficionado of Spanish New Mexican folk art, Dixon cherished the old woodwork around the fireplaces, the handmade screen doors, and simple Territorial-style windows, and he assembled the household goods of a modest country New Mexican home from the Spanish, Mexican, and Territorial periods of New Mexico's history. Tinwork became his special interest. In

A salvaged corner fireplace facade from the late 19th century dominates the entry at the Dixon home, *right*. Northern New Mexico's Hispanic carpenters gained access to sawmill lumber in the 19th century. With sufficient wood for their craft, they covered old adobe corner fireplaces and added woodwork throughout the home. Late Victorian decorative devices gave a sense of playfulness and lightness to plain adobe homes.

the late 1980s, Dixon was able to acquire all of the holdings of a legendary gifted but irascible tinworker of the Revival period named Robert Woodman, who worked on Canyon Road in nearby Santa Fe in the 1930s and 40s. In Woodman's studio, Dixon found the craftsman's tools and patterns. As an artist Dixon was able to appreciate the importance of his find. He began by repairing and completing Woodman's work and then went on to become an important contributor to the field, working in tin himself and as a scholar and coauthor of the pioneering work on the subject, *New Mexican Tinwork, 1840–1940.*

Solid wooden doors were typical of the previous generation of woodwork, when pine had to be hand hewn and adzed, *right.* The cow skull above the doorway and against the adobe wall has become emblematic of New Mexico through the paintings of Georgia O'Keeffe. Painted Mexican chairs flank the door.

In addition to tin frames, craftsmen in Mexico and New Mexico fashioned fancy tin *nichos,* which were used to hold a figure of a saint, *opposite.* The tinwork of New Mexico was bolder in style compared to the tinwork of Mexico, which is delicate in detail. A colonial *trastero* (cupboard) is filled with treasured folk art objects, *right.* Included among the treasures are art objects, tinwork, Pueblo pottery, Mexican folk art, and a nativity scene by Marie Romero Cash.

One corner of the *sala grande* (living room) of the Dixon home is filled with some of the tools typical of the colonial and Mexican periods of the Southwest, *left.* Hispanic colonists had to make do with materials at hand, even fashioning tool handles out of tree roots. Iron in particular was in short supply. Tin frames, an earthenware Mexican platter, and a wooden bowl are set upon a fine old Mexican chest, *opposite.* Such chests held the important linens of the household and were part of a woman's dowry. The doorway looks to a chapel beyond. In outlying areas, homes frequently had a separate chapel for the use of the household and neighbors.

Plates from Old Mexico line a New Mexican-made rack, *opposite.* In moderate climates, the Spanish house was constructed around a central courtyard to bring the outside inside, *right.* The table and chairs are carefully placed under the protection of the *portal* (porch). Within the courtyards simple old-fashioned flowers grew in profusion for use in the house, *opposite.* A venerable cactus and vine grow in the courtyard of the Dixon home, *below.*

A TOUCH OF ELEGANCE

Born in poverty, tinwork's purpose is to introduce a touch of luxury and a flash of light into places where there is often a conspicuous absence of both. In New Mexico in the 19th century, skilled hands transformed discarded U.S. Army tin containers into frames, chandeliers, candle sconces, boxes, and a host of other decorative items. Having lacked the most basic necessities for centuries, the Spanish New Mexican housewife eagerly displayed these humble objects of beauty. Into the frames, tinworkers pressed treasured chromolithographic prints of the saints; for a touch of elegance, they added bits of wallpaper behind the glass.

Among the poorer parishes, in which silver could be little afforded, all manner of religious objects were fashioned of tin, from the saint's crown to the box for the host. By the late 19th and early 20th centuries, tinwork was accepted as part of the regional style of decoration, not just a poor substitute for silver. By the 1930s and 1940s, workshops had been established to supply tinwork for hotels and homes. A few great craftsmen keep the tradition alive today.

Crosses of tin and glass with decorative backgrounds of wallpaper, embroidery, and handpainted flowers are examples of the work of Emilio and Senaida Romero, *left*. An image of the Virgin is set off by a tin frame made by the Romeros, *opposite*. The *colcha* embroidery behind the glass of the frames is by Senaida Romero.

THE PAST PRESERVED

The life that Al Luckett pursues in his house on Upper Canyon Road in Santa Fe is part of the Santa Fe of the past, a world in which self-sufficiency was crucial and faith was paramount. Luckett's collection of *santos* illuminates a time in New Mexico when the saints were as necessary to daily life as the chairs and the plow. Many of Luckett's *santos* were made by a single *santero*, José Benito Ortega. Within Santa Fe and in a number of mountain villages during the 18th and 19th centuries, individual *santeros* worked to fill the commissions of the many households and parishes that needed religious imagery. José Benito Ortega was among the last in this legacy of local *santeros*. Working in the mountains, in the town of Mora, he apparently specialized in large figures of Christ, a number of examples of which are in the Luckett collection. Besides the saint figures, Luckett has judiciously collected Spanish New Mexican colonial furniture, tinwork, Rio Grande textiles, as well as paintings from the productive years of American painting in Santa Fe and Taos of the 1920s and 1930s.

The simplicity and unity of the West's Hispanic heritage have tremendous appeal for collectors like Al Luckett, who appreciate the rarity of a harmoniously integrated life.

A standing Christ figure attributed to José Benito Ortega stands next to a painted chest of 19th-century New Mexican origin, *left.* On the chest are a Holy Family attributed to Fray Andrés García. A collection of New Mexican folk art in the Luckett home, *right,* includes a standing Christ figure and a crucifix attributed to 19th-century New Mexican *santero* José Benito Ortega. The 1926 painting of *Penitentes* is by Western artist Peter Hurd. On the table is a carving by Celso Gallegos, a folk artist working in Agua Fría, New Mexico, in the 1920s.

Below, a New Mexican *retablo* of the Trinity stands before a *metraca* (noisemaker) that would have been used during the Lenten season to call people to worship; the *metraca* is placed upon a *jerga,* a twill-woven textile of Spanish New Mexico which was used for everything from sacking material to floor coverings. A large painted New Mexican *trastero* of the turn of the century, *right,* stands in the entryway. Large case pieces made of milled lumber helped to hold the household clothing in adobe homes, notorious for their lack of closets.

Pieces from an extensive collection of New Mexican *santos* and folk art of the 18th and 19th centuries sit upon large chests in the Luckett house. In the group, *right,* San Antonio de Padua is at the left, Santa Librada in the center, and Archangel San Rafael is at the right. The *olla* (pot) next to the archangel is of copper. Above the chest is a *repisa* (shelf), which holds the type of *retablos* that were found in the homes of New Mexico. The large grain chest, which holds *bultos* of various advocations of the Virgin, *below right,* also has a rare *bulto* of Saint Christopher holding the Christ Child. The crosses of wood decorated with straw are 19th-century New Mexican, while the delicate crucifix at the far right is probably Mexican.

The dining room, *left,* is filled with New Mexican furniture, especially chairs. Chairs were the most common piece of furniture in the 18th and 19th centuries in the northern frontier of New Spain. The painting of Ranchos de Taos church above the chair is by Emil Bisttram. The corner fireplace beyond holds further examples of New Mexican religious folk art of the 19th century. The lock and hasp detail, *opposite,* is from a New Mexican *trastero* (cupboard). Even such simple iron hardware was rare in the northern frontier, where all metal was at a premium.

CLASSIC FRONTIER FURNITURE

At the turn of the century in New Mexico, all of the cultural gains Spanish colonists had made over the centuries were in danger of being lost to the forces of change from the East. To counterbalance the Anglo influences that were making Southwestern communities look more and more like towns back East, activist residents worked to revive Spanish colonial architecture and decorative arts. Furniture was a

Guest quarters at Ghost Ranch, Abiquiu, New Mexico, photographed by T. Harmon Parkhurst in 1935, featured Hispanic-style furnishings, *opposite.* Solid and square in proportion, much Hispanic furniture has an almost medieval quality. The unfinished, plain surfaces and simple geometric decorative motifs add to the feeling of solidity. Revival-style pieces such as the chest with drawers in the home of Elizabeth and Jim McGordy, *right,* retain the massive proportions of early Hispanic furniture, with the addition of an all-over adzed surface that highlights the woods used. Above the chest, a *repisa* holds a collection of Pueblo pottery; on the chest are two Virgins of Guadalupe *bultos* and a woodcarving by Taos woodcarver Patrocinio Barela.

primary focus of attention. Preservationists gathered photographic documentation of 18th- and 19th-century colonial furniture and donated chairs, tables, benches, *trasteros* (cupboards), and other historic pieces to historical societies and museums. With the completion of a few significant Revival-style buildings, furniture was designed and manufactured to fill these public spaces. Furniture made for the Museum of Fine Arts in Santa Fe, built in 1918, employed elements of the past yet departed stylistically from the originals. The

The *trastero* and bench made by Taos furniture maker Greg Flores are seen in the Martínez Hacienda in Taos, *above left* and *left*. The hacienda is a perfect backdrop to Flores's furniture, which exemplifies all of the qualities of Hispanic New Mexican furniture. Dwellings of the past had few furnishings and those that were available served direct, practical functions and were always unpretentious. Flores strives to maintain the integrity of the old styles with his furniture, such as the straight and humble chair, *opposite*.

overall look of the furniture tended to be more massive to match the needs of the larger rooms, and the carving was painted instead of left in natural wood. A number of furniture types, such as sideboards, beds, desks, magazine racks, and nightstands, which had not existed in the past, were also adapted in the new Revival style. As part of the Works Progress Administration during the Depression, workshops in northern New Mexico put craftsmen to work: the making of furniture was among the more successful enterprises. Colonial New Mexican furniture, like the early Pilgrim furniture of the East Coast, is exceedingly rare and most fine pieces are now carefully housed in public collections. Collectors are turning to the Revival furniture and crafts and to new craftsmen who are working in the genre today.

The kitchen of the Martínez Hacienda was barely furnished. Chairs, such as the one by Greg Flores, *opposite,* were very rare and were often reserved for special guests. Household members often sat on little stools called *tarimas.* Large *trasteros* like the one by Greg Flores, *right,* held the family's valuables and would have been found only in the most prosperous homes. The absence of heavy iron locks and latches or of fancy painted decoration is typical of New Mexican furniture.

RIO GRANDE WEAVINGS

When the Spanish arrived in the New World they brought sheep, transforming millennia of weaving traditions among the indigenous people of North America. In the Southwest, the Navajo became sheep raisers and weavers without parallel. Less known but perhaps as productive were the highly skilled Spanish New Mexican weavers. They produced wool weavings, often called Rio Grandes after the area where the tradition emerged, in the early years of settlement up until the beginning of the 20th century. Unlike Native Americans, the Spanish worked on massive horizontal or treadle looms. Weaving was for the most part men's work, although wool preparation, spinning, and carding were done by women.

Throughout the colonial era,

A mosaic of details shows off 18th- and 19th-century Spanish New Mexican textiles from collections at the Museum of International Folk Art, Museum of New Mexico, in Santa Fe, *left.* These wool blankets were made for centuries by Spanish colonists, not only for local use but also for trade with Mexico. Simple bands and stripes, as well as more intricate geometric designs, are woven on large treadle looms. The large embroidery, called a *colcha,* also from the Museum of International Folk Art, *opposite,* was done in New Mexico. The wool embroidery is placed on a background of woven wool called *sabanilla.* Designs are most often floral.

blankets and other textiles were woven in great quantities, not only for use by the colonists but in exchange for currency or manufactured goods needed by the struggling colony from the large cities of Mexico. The most common design for utilitarian blankets featured simple bands and stripes in brown, white, and indigo blue. More elaborately designed textiles used as garments were often woven in a pattern associated with Saltillo, Mexico.

Besides blankets, weavers also made lengths of *sabanilla*, a plain wool sheeting fabric for mattresses and other useful items. *Sabanilla* also served as the backing fabric for a type of embroidery called *colcha*. Seamstresses stitched floral and geometric designs on these delicate colonial textiles used as bedspreads or as altar cloths.

With the advent of aniline dyes, the Spanish New Mexican weavers exploited the newly available colors in an explosion of bright reds, greens, purples, and yellows. The later blankets have no stylistic antecedents and remain a unique legacy of the Spanish of New Mexico.

A *colcha* called a Carson *colcha* after the location where it was made in the 1930s, *opposite,* portrays the members of the Penitente brotherhood in the religious act of self-flagellation and a crucifix at top and bottom. Carson *colchas* were made for sale to Anglo-American collectors who were eager for textiles with Spanish motifs. The embroidery, *right,* is also called *colcha,* but is embroidered on simple, machine-made cotton sheeting rather than wool. This type of textile would have been made after the opening of the Santa Fe Trail, when manufactured goods were first available.

The bedroom of weaver Teresa Archuleta-Sagel, seen at work, *above,* and her husband, Jim Sagel, is filled with the types of traditional Mexican and New Mexican textiles that serve as an inspiration for the contemporary weaver, *left.* New Mexican homeowners, the couple built their house by hand; the bedroom is the most recent addition. Teresa learned to weave from famed traditionalist Doña Agueda Martínez of Medanles, New Mexico. Unlike her mentor, Teresa gives personal meaning to each of her textiles through specific titles and often poems that reflect the textile's meaning to the weaver. Among her pieces are *Raindrop Saltillo, top right;* and *My Lost Heart Is Venus, bottom right.* Her yarn, combs, spindles, and other tools fill the basket, *center right.*

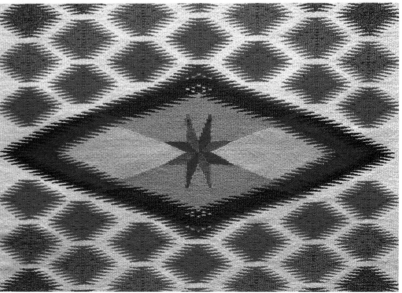

Formally, a fiesta is a festival or feast in honor of an important saint's day or a celebration of an apparition of the Virgin, a great historical event, or a day of independence. In practice, fiesta is a riot with minimal organization and loads of history—a time to let it all go, salute the old, welcome the new, follow the tradition, raise the cup, and dance until you drop. Loud music, big crowds, too much to eat and drink, staying up late—these are the excesses that characterize a good fiesta.

Though fiestas vary from town to town, the underlying reason for the celebration has remained the same over the

A group of singers from Santa Fiesta of about 1925, *above,* wear Mexican costumes, which were popular at the time. The De Vargas Pageant on Santa Fe's Plaza was captured by Jesse Nusbaum in 1911, *right.* In the early years of the 20th century Santa Fe fiestas regularly included participants from various tribal groups in the area. As time went on Native Americans refused to participate in an event that celebrated their own conquest.

centuries—to forget everyday cares and anxieties, and to feel free from worry, if only for a day or two. In Santa Fe the fiesta is a celebration of the Reconquest of New Mexico by Don Diego de Vargas and a thanksgiving to the Virgin of the Conquest—*La Conquistadora.* What began as a solemn religious celebration in the 18th century has become an excuse for the entire city to pour into the plaza for a long weekend that includes such secular events as the Hysterical-Historical Parade, the Pet Parade, dances, and musical events. At Mesilla, New Mexico, young dancers dressed in Mexican folk costumes dance the folkloric steps of the liberating Latin music of Mexico.

By far some of the most unusual and original fiesta fashions in Santa Fe were the dresses made from fine old Mexican shawls, *opposite, left,* and *above.* Often called *mantones de Manila,* or Chinese shawls, these were highly treasured heirlooms that earned their nickname in the era of the Manila galleons. The Fiesta Chorus of 1925 performs in front of the Palace of the Governors, Santa Fe, *top.*

The revived fiesta in Mesilla, New Mexico, not only serves as an opportunity for the community to gather but has also brought forth a new generation of dancers and their brilliant costumes based upon folkloric dances from Mexico. A lively swirl of skirts creates a blur of color, *top.* A dancer helps a friend keep her wardrobe intact for the festivities, *above.* A group of beautiful youngsters pose proudly in their fiesta costumes, *right.* Scenes from fiestas in Santa Fe and Mesilla give a sense of the colorful action of these events, *following pages.*

CHARROS

The world's first large stock-breeding ranches were in Mexico. These large haciendas not only bred fine cattle but also produced some of the greatest horsemen the world has ever known. For many years after the Conquest, Indians were forbidden to ride on horseback. Later, on the large, rural haciendas, the law became impractical, since no one was available to work the cattle. With the merging of the peasant Indian and horse came the daring athleticism of the *vaquero* (cowboy) and *charro* (horseman), who rounded up wild cattle using many techniques unknown in the Old World. When foreign invaders attacked Mexican soil in the 19th century the *charros* played a special patriotic role, often riding into the midst of fire and pulling over cannon with their accurate lariat skills.

By the late 19th century the skills of the *charro* had been well recognized in his own country, and like the cowboy the mythology and romanticization of the *charros* had begun in earnest both in Mexico and elsewhere. *Charro* groups traveled to Spain to show off their skills, and Buffalo Bill added *charros* to his repertoire for

Although the *charro* primarily spotlights the prowess of the *vaquero*, women also participate. At the Fiesta de los Vaqueros in Tucson, a group of riders sit sidesaddle, preparing to perform, *left*. Their costumes are similar to the full-skirted, colorful wardrobe of the folkloric dancers in fiestas. The riding skills of the *charras* are as exquisite and demanding as those of the men, yet they are always executed with the femininity so highly prized in Latin cultures— athleticism tempered with grace.

shows traveling as far away as New York City. Pulp novels featuring the macho *charro* and the simpering *ranchera* maiden, became models for equally stereotypical movies made in the 1930s. With the decline of the large rural haciendas, the *charros* took to the cities. Most large Mexican cities maintain an active *charro* association that sponsors weekend events for lawyers, doctors, and other city dwellers who wish to act out the rural life of the 19th-century *charro*. Competitions and public performances, which parallel the American cowboy's rodeo, are offered in the *lienzo* (arena). Like the rodeo, the *jaripeo* (show) is a wonderful opportunity to display both the costumes and the skills of the *charro*.

The roping skills of the Mexican *vaquero* are celebrated in the *charrería,* here by a *charro* performing at the Fiesta de los Vaqueros, *left.* In the *lienzo* (arena) in Aguascalientes, Mexico, a group of *charros* chat while waiting their turn to perform, *opposite.* This particular *charrería* was an international competition that drew riders from as far away as Argentina.

PART TWO

COWBOY CULTURE

AMERICA'S ROMANCE WITH THE HEROES OF THE PLAINS

The American cowboy has been exalted to the stature of a demi-god in part because of the very nature of his work. Anyone willing to labor long hours in all types of weather with large and often dangerous animals for little or no pay deserves at the very least to be applauded as a hero. Without the horse, the cowboy would have been no more than another farm worker, but with his mount, the caretaker of cattle was transformed into a mythic figure. Together, cowboy and horse survived the rigors of long days on the trail in blistering summers and bone-chilling winters. In return for the steadfast toil of an initially unwilling partner, the cowboy celebrated his horse in poetry and song, and with the tribute of handsomely adorned saddles, bridles, and other gear.

Much of the gear, along with the cowboy's working methods and the very concept of ranching, came from the other America—Latin America and Mexico. Large haciendas in northern Mexico and later in Texas served as training grounds for American ranchers and cattlemen. Open grazing, for example, the basis for American ranching practices, derived from the Hispanic agricultural custom of setting aside communal lands for livestock. The roundup, the "Western" saddle, the broadbrimmed hat, the lariat, the branding iron, and even the breed of cattle—all came from the Spanish Americans.

The transference of this culture from Mexican *vaquero* to American cowboy occurred with remarkable rapidity in the mid-19th century, and declined just as quickly—leaving a sense of nostalgia for the Old West a mere 50 years after the cowboy helped invent it. Perhaps this fast-paced rise and fall had something to do with cowboying itself—it just isn't a life you can live for very long. A cowboy's requirements are indeed superhuman: great physical stamina, isolation from towns and hearths, and an array of demanding, sometimes acrobatic skills. What remains hard work today was extremely hard work a century ago when Americans fell seriously in love with the image of the cowboy. It was an image of young men mounted on beautiful horses riding off into the limitless grasslands, enduring hardship and deprivation and conquering obstacles through sheer physical mastery. This image has all the elements for the creation of heros.

Less often eulogized but crucial to the cowboy was ranching. Not to be confused with cowboying, the more prosaic life of the rancher involved such wearisome bonds as the ownership of private property, including stock, wife and children, mortgages, and balance sheets. Once the open range began to disappear (which was almost as soon as it was recognized), ownership—and fencing—of large tracts of land became essential. Ranching and the accompanying cowboy spread northward from the border areas of California, Texas, Arizona, and New Mexico to Montana, Wyoming, and Canada as the appetite for grazing land increased.

Cattle grazing, as any environmentalist will quickly attest, places heavy demands upon the land. The rancher's needs were often in conflict with the needs of those who had come before him—the Native Americans—and those who followed—the homesteader and farmer. Competition for the land, and for water, became the primary drama of the West, and the seemingly vast frontier was the stage

Archie Wittick, in a double exposure by his father, Ben Wittick, entitled "High" pokes fun at the cardsharps of the day.

on which it was enacted. Ranching was doomed to be under a state of siege from the outset since it was by nature self-contradictory: on the one hand cattlemen needed to open the land and settle it for development; on the other, they had to keep it uninhabited and free for grazing. There could be only one wave of pure ranching and cowboying—the first. After this Golden Age, it was all conflict, fencing, and shrinking frontiers.

Despite the conflicts, ranch life had its relaxed moments. There was time to get together for picnics and barbecues and most of all for the annual or semiannual or Friday afternoon rodeo. Rodeo, an event that descended from the Hispanic *charrería*, pushes both the skills and bravery of the cowboy to the limit. Most of the events of the rodeo relate to the skills needed by the working cowboy. The rodeo was—and is—also the opportunity for cowboys to compete and show off—a great saddle or pair of chaps, a well-bred and well-trained horse, and the winning belt buckle from last year's rodeo. Dusty, tattered work clothes give way to crisp shirts and jeans, special boots, and spotless hats.

The modern rodeo is in effect where the style of the cowboy became public spectacle. At the rodeo, dress, movement, stance, and attitude all seem to blend into a ritual celebration of the romance of cowboying. The crease of jeans, the elbows resting back on the fence rail, the intense concentration of the rider as he straps himself onto the bull, the constant banter between the clown and the announcer—all are as stylized as were the ancient Roman gladiator contests. Rodeoing does not pay very well—in fact, it never even covers the costs of the nights on the road, equipment, horses, and doctor's bills, even for those talented enough to spend a few short years at the top. But like the life it celebrates, rodeoing is just too good for many cowboy performers to give up.

Rodeoing may have become show business; ranching, which requires huge investments in land and cattle, is now firmly a part of agribusiness. Ironically, only the dude ranch—properly categorized as resort management rather than ranching—preserves the flavor of the ranch life of the past. In fact, the dude virtually saved the Old West ranch from oblivion. Not along after the Wild West show and the pulp Western novel introduced city

Cowboys rope a calf for branding in a classic tableau of Western life, from New Mexico in the 1940s.

folk to the life of the cowboy, a few ranches in the Northwest began taking in paying visitors. The rustic ranch houses built to hold those weekend cowboys may have been far from the realities of the bunkhouse, but they further popularized not only the cowboy's life but also the look of the West. The wagon wheel chandeliers, trophy heads, Navajo rugs, and lodgepole pine furniture that typically decorated the public rooms of the dude ranch are now as much part of the Western style as the simple decor of the working ranch. The fortunes of dude ranching rise and fall with the public's fascination with the myth of the West, but as long as the cowboy remains as one of America's favorite folk heros, the ranch will be a treasured part of our heritage.

Women joined the rank of gunslingers and toughs in the West and enjoyed the glamour of the costume and the gear along with the men.

After cowboys began to appear in the movies now called "classic" Westerns, and on television from the morning through the evening, they achieved a new mythical renown that spread not only to every region of the United States but also to every corner of the world. No matter that cowboy life was actually difficult and often decidedly tedious, our national consciousness glamorized cowboy culture until it came to symbolize the epitome of individual freedom. Even now as we begin to revisit our history with a fresh and often critical eye, an America without the cowboy is as hard to imagine as America without the Pilgrims and the founding fathers.

WORKING CATTLE

Sturdy Polled Angus, Herefords, and Shorthorns have replaced the wild and rangy Longhorns and Chinos of the past as the source of livelihood for Western cattlemen, but the hopes and dreams are much the same. After the Civil War poor and desperate men went West to find their fortunes from wild cattle. A growing taste for beef in the East and Europe, as well as in the Far West, made cattle driving a feasible get-rich-quick scheme for those who owned little but a horse and saddle. The true "wild cattle," the Bison, which had once filled the Plains by the millions, had been almost exterminated in less than a decade, leaving enormous tracts of grassland, or open range, available to the newly formed group of cattlemen. The hoof trails—Chisholm, Goodnight, and others—and the great trail drives of thousands of cattle to shipping or packing locations such as Dodge City, marked but a brief moment in the history of the American West, yet the romance and danger of these drives has forever colored our vision of the West. There was big money to be made—in some cases enough money so

May in the Texas Panhandle is roundup time for the cowboy. Gary and Monte lead the cattle to a holding area, so that the calves can be branded. The dense scrub and tricky gullies and washes of the Panhandle can make roundup an exhausting chore. Despite the intensity of the work, cowboys at the Pitchfork Ranch, near Guthrie, Texas, look forward to spring and branding when the real work of cowboying begins. Once in the corral Gary begins the sorting process, *above.*

that cattlemen could settle down upon huge ranches and fence and protect their land. By the 1800s the "nesters" and "sodbusters" had irrevocably changed attitudes toward the land, and soon barbed wire crisscrossed what once had been open country. Well-bred Angus and other breeds replaced the less civilized cattle of before, and the railroad made the protracted and dangerous trail drives a pleasant relic of a bygone era.

Water propels an eager herd forward. Live water is a necessity for large-scale cattle operations, and drought and water disputes have brought the downfall of many ranching empires. Most cattle ranching in Texas is on private land rather than through leases on federal properties, as it is in other states. In the early years of Texas ranching, owners realized the need to establish large properties in order to protect their rights to grazing and water.

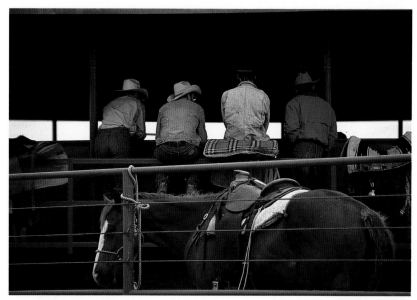

Horsebreaking was once a brutal experience for both horse and rider. At the famed 6666 Ranch in the Texas Panhandle, a specialist in horsebreaking educates the cowboys in the modern, gentler method of taming and training wild or young horses, which is based on studies of animal behavior and behavior modification, *left, top,* and *above.* Increasingly, ranching and cowboying depends upon the ranch management courses at the universities to aid in developing sound methods of stock and range management.

BRANDING

The branding of cattle in the New World is almost as old as the arrival of the species from Europe in the second decade of the 16th century. Hernán Cortés had his brand registered, and early laws in Mexico required the registration of brands with the government. Each region or territory kept brand books, and individuals might have a number of brands registered in their name. Stamp irons, which burned the design into the beast's hide, became the most common method of getting the job done. Unbranded cattle were routinely rounded up and claimed in the unfenced and unfettered West of the 19th century. Cattle raids back and forth across the borders did little to foster a sense of neighborliness with Mexico—a situation that kept the borderland volatile right into the 20th century.

Branding occurs most often in the spring when calves are rounded up for branding, dehorning, vaccination, and castration—a series of tasks that a well-coordinated, highly skilled group of cowboys can carry out in a matter of minutes.

Branding at the Pitchfork Ranch is still an annual spring event. After rounding up the herd and separating out the calves, *above left* and *right*, cowboys brand the calves for identification, *center left*, and inoculate them, *bottom left* and *inset*.

COWBOY COOKING

The wages could be fair and the companionship good, but the cowboy measured his happiness by the caliber of his meals. The cook, with his chuck wagon, accompanied the work crew and carried all the supplies and bedding, as well as the food and the camp kit necessary to prepare it. The wagon was the center of life for the working cowboy, and his appe-tite matched the length of his hard days on the trail. Cooks were legendary for their irasci-ble temperaments—everyone, including bosses, stayed clear of the cook's territory. Since the quality of what little free time the cowboys might have de-pended greatly upon the cook —the extra pies he might pre-pare and the quality and clean-liness of the meals—good cooks were well paid and highly prized. Cowboys might refuse work when they knew the cooking would be poor. Meals were simple—beans, bacon, biscuits, coffee, pies, and per-haps beef—but the work con-

"Mex John," a chuck wagon chef, makes pies from the back of his turn-of-the-century chuck wagon, *above.* The simple back flap of this wagon can be used for both preparation and food service. At the Grant-Kohrs Ranch in Montana, a chuck wagon awaits the food cooked over a campfire, *right.*

ditions were difficult. Cooks established camp ahead of the crew, located fresh water and gathered fuel, and prepared the victuals for ravenously hungry men.

The chuck wagon is a pure American invention made to suit long months of life on the range. Said to have been the invention of famed cattleman Charles Goodnight, the chuck wagon had a large cupboard built between the sideboards at the back of the wagon. Secured drawers held many of the cook's supplies, and a back flap was lowered and propped up to make a work space. Wagons still follow the cowboys at branding time; many a ranch is loath to give up this great old tradition.

Water was often not available for cooking or drinking so one of the important functions of the chuck wagon was hauling water to the campsites of the cowboys, *right*. *Below*, a chuck wagon lunch for the cowboys of the 6666 Ranch in the Texas Panhandle.

Cooking over an open fire was always a challenge, especially when fuel was hard to find. Simple, indestructible iron Dutch ovens, skillets, and coffee pots, *left,* were essential to camp cooking. *Above,* a group of cowboys at the 6666 Ranch enjoy a meal that brings back memories of trail-driving days.

A RANCHING LEGACY

Western ranches were as different as the many different kinds of Western terrain in which they were found. When a rancher first settled in, his primary needs were for water and a corral. Live water was and is the major issue of the West—a single steer might need 25 gallons per day—and many a man has lost his life over a water dispute. If a source of water was not readily available, tanks were built for stock and wells were dug, often by hand. Homes might be of sod, adobe, logs, or stone depending on what materials were at hand. Corrals, like homes, were built using local materials. With the advent of barbed wire in the 1870s, fencing animals became simpler, but the disputes caused by the new practice were often resolved as fiercely as those over water.

This view from the past, through a porch and picket fence to a buckboard beyond, is at the Ranching Heritage Center in Lubbock, Texas, *left*.

Refinements such as clapboard siding came to Texas as soon as milled lumber was available, *left.* A bucket and pail, *below,* were simple and efficient means of cleaning up for the entire family and all of the ranch hands. Cowboys looked forward to the ranch or town for a chance to get cleaned up after days in the saddle.

The variety of outbuildings that eventually made up the ranch complex depended greatly upon how the ranch functioned and where it was located. Many ranches gradually added on barns, stables, storage facilities, and bunkhouses as need arose and resources allowed. At the Ranching Heritage Center in Lubbock, Texas, over 30 structures from historic ranches in Texas have been brought together to show both the variety and the architectural evolution of the ranch. From early dugout buildings and primitive log cabins, the most prosperous ranches boasted frame homes and even Victorian extravaganzas.

Back at the ranch, women struggled to maintain a semblance of order and civilization under difficult circumstances. Kitchens consisted of little more than a cook stove, table, and a few utensils, *above left,* yet produced immense meals for large extended families and hungry ranch hands. The dresser in the ranch bedroom, *left,* would have been ordered through mail-order catalogues. Sears & Roebuck became the most famous and successful of the mail-order businesses and furnished entire homes. The sewing machine was a luxury longed for by every housewife, since it gave her the opportunity to clothe her family and add curtains to the bedroom, *right.*

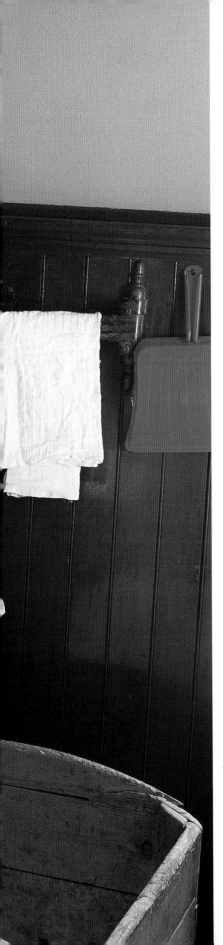

A top-of-the-line Monarch stove is the focal point of the kitchen in a house at the Grant-Kohrs Ranch, *left.* Nearby, the woodbox sits empty, unimaginable in the days when the cook fed both family and ranch hands. A half-dugout home at the Ranching Heritage Center, *right,* shows the early stages of ranch life when homes were built under a variety of difficult circumstances. A partly subterranean home offered insulation, but was never truly free of dirt. Later, as the ranch prospered, a new ranch house would be built and such buildings might be converted to other uses. Homes were uniformly modest and cozy as was this turn-of-the-century ranch home, *below right,* where the kitchen stove is a few short feet from the bedroom beyond. A panorama of ranch signs, *following pages,* shows the variety of welcomes to Western homes.

DIXIE DUDE RANCH

"YOUR HOME ON THE RANGE"

IN BANDERA HILL COUNTRY

WORTH

REGISTERED TEXAS LONGHORNS

WILSON

SPEAR 2 RANCH

RALPH & LIB
CORTESE

GRISSOM

BROWNS
RIVERBEND RANCH

BACK AT THE RANCH

When Augusta Kohrs died at the age of 96 in 1945, the ranch she and her husband, Conrad, had developed was already legendary. Its history spanned and influenced almost the entire history of ranching on the High Plains of Montana. Taking on this sizable property from Johnny Grant, who established the ranch in the Deer Lodge Valley in the 1850s, the Kohrs immediately began the process of improving and expanding it. Conrad Kohr's success hinged both on his willingness to diversify his holdings and on his development of fine breeding stock. When disaster eliminated countless ranches in the murderous winters of 1886 and 1887, Kohr's superior and well-sheltered stock not only survived but, in the absence of

The stake-and-rider fence was popular among ranches where timber was plentiful, *opposite.* The main advantages of this fencing were that it required no post holes be dug and that the top rail was very difficult for cattle to dislodge. The main house of the Grant-Kohrs Ranch served not only as the family home, *above right,* but as a center to house and feed the many guests who came to the ranch. As the ranch prospered new wings were added to the great house, and various outbuildings, such as this buggy shed, *right,* were built to handle different functions. Over the years the ranch added new equipment, operations, and buildings, such as the feedlot and chicken coop and a variety of farm equipment, *following pages.*

competition, increased dramatically in value. In the heyday of the ranch, the Kohrs ran cattle on over 1 million acres in four states and Canada.

The ranch house in Deer Lodge, run by Augusta, was widely considered to be the finest in the territory. Victorian furniture and other luxuries arrived on the same trains that were used to ship the cattle out, and the Kohrs's home became a cultural and political center for the region. Out back, the bunkhouse represented another aspect of Montana society—the cowboys. Though relatively plain compared to the main house, the bunkhouse and communal dining area were a veritable paradise for the working cowboy.

Sturdy chinked-log buildings housed the most valuable animals on the ranch. Kohrs had separate stallion barns, *below,* and a nearby thoroughbred barn, *right.* Oxen were used in the early years of ranching for heavy work but were later replaced by draft horses. These stock and their sturdy barns were crucial, since they added considerable revenue and stability to the ranching operation.

Careful notching on corners of log buildings was essential for strong, level, and weathertight construction. A well-built log house, carefully chinked and maintained, can last for generations, *above* and *right.*

A WRITER'S REST

It is a simple ranch, not a fussy showplace, but a home to settle in and watch the snow fall and admire the seasons as they come and go.

Like those who love it, it is without pretense. The ranch that the renowned Western writer Louis L'Amour bought for himself and his family was once a little stage stop, a traveler's rest along the road that traversed southern Colorado in the days when journeys were long and hard. It became a traveler's rest for the writer who had traveled so much of the world and had reported on his explorations and observations of that life of adventure. The road follows different routes now, and the log house and old barn are protected from the world of intrusions by high ridges. Inside, the exposed hewn logs of the old stage stop set the tone for a romantic yet humble home in the West. There are few visual reminders that this was the home of one of the world's most popular writers of all time.

Set in a valley deep in December snows lies the old stage stop home restored and renovated by Louis and Kathy L'Amour, *opposite.* Homes, outbuildings, and barns in the mountainous areas of Colorado have steeply pitched roofs so that snow does not accumulate on the roof and cause it to collapse. A simple rail, or zigzag, fence divides the property and provides a picturesque touch to the backdrop of hills and forests, *right.*

BANDANNAS

For the early cowboys, the bandanna had a single important function—to protect the neck against the elements in a time when workshirts lacked adequate collars.

The term *bandanna* derives from *bandhana*, a tie-dying technique from India, where the bold design of the cowboy kerchief originated. Eventually mass-produced in textile printing factories, the red or blue bandanna might be the only bit of color in the cowhand's otherwise drab wardrobe. Bandannas and neckerchiefs were used both in Europe and America during the 18th and 19th centuries as a medium to carry a message—sometimes political, instructive, religious, or decorative. Both men and women used them in countless humdrum ways in their dress and daily lives, and most were discarded. Special events, political happenings, and tourism often prompted an outpouring of new bandanna styles, and newly effective advertising.

Once a necessary item of clothing, the bandanna evolved into a feature of the cowboy costume. Although shirt collars are now sufficiently wide to shield a cowboy's neck from the sun, a Western outfit is still incomplete without a bandanna.

One of the all-time popular motifs of cowboying, the bucking bronco or "Ride'em Cowboy" image, has become emblematic of the cowboy and appears on everything from bandannas to bedspreads. The bandannas of Mary Hunt Kahlenberg, a lifetime collector in Santa Fe, reveal the variety and popularity of this and other cowboy motifs, *left*, *opposite*, and *following pages*.

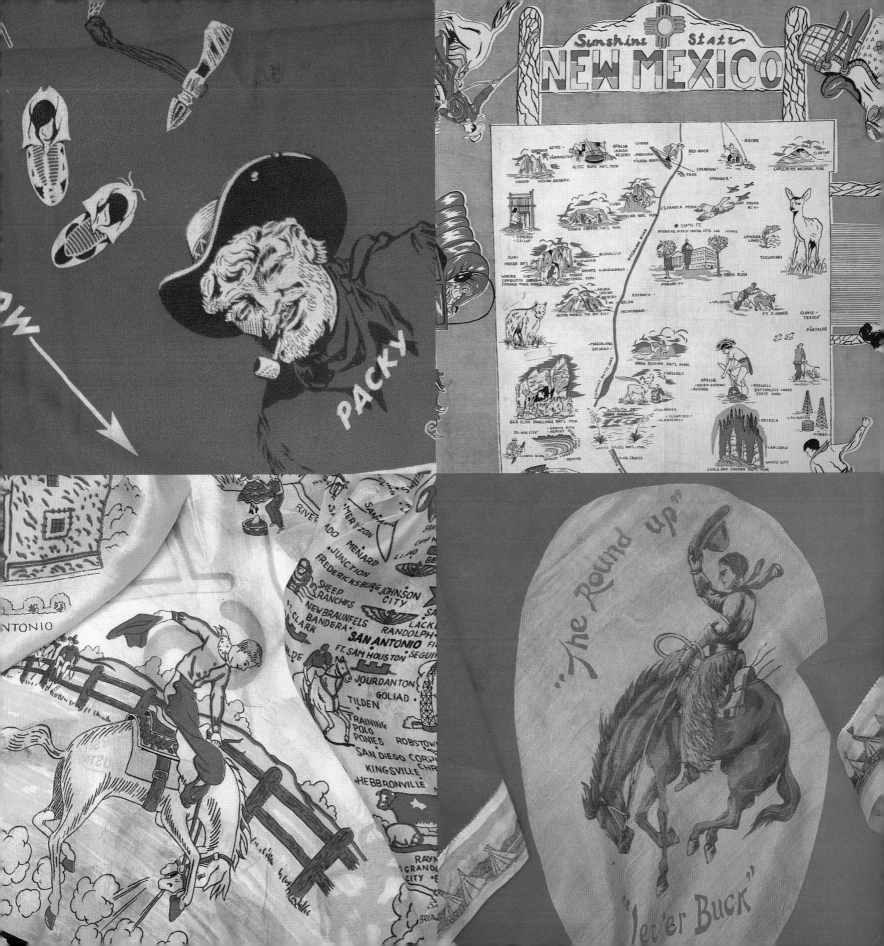

COWBOY HEADGEAR

Not so very long ago Western hatters kept every client's hat size on file, and handmade every hat with brim and crease to order. Starting with fine felted fur, they steamed, molded, and trimmed the hats, then added the desired final touches. The finest hats were made of beaver; the belly of the beaver was the best of the pelt. Hats were a necessity in the direct sun or bitter cold of the range, and no cowboy rode out without one, even though a good hat might represent close to a month's wages. When a hat finally succumbed to the wear and tear of heat, rain, dust, and cattle hooves,

The winner of the World's Most Beat-Up Hat Contest at the local rodeo is proudly displayed with a well-used pair of chaps at the Pitchfork Ranch near Guthrie, Texas, *opposite.* Hats modeled by Bob Moorehouse, the manager at Pitchfork Ranch, *above right;* two young cowboys watching the action at Pitchfork, *above far right* and *below right,* and "Stoney" Wellman, *below far right,* have seen somewhat less wear and tear.

the cowboy headed back to his favorite hatmaker, and ordered another.

In the West today, the local hatmaker has been replaced by big manufacturers, such as Resistol and Stetson. John B. Stetson, the famed hat manufacturer of Philadelphia, first designed and then mass-produced cowboy hats in the 1870s following a trip out West. Before that time cowboys, like their *vaquero* counterparts, wore sombreros, and it was this form that so clearly influenced Stetson.

Clee Woods, a turn-of-the-century cowboy, had his portrait taken wearing his brand-new hat, *left*. Working hats, like their owners, take a lot of abuse. The soft, felted materials of the original hat are lost in layers of sweat and grime and are punctuated with a few extra holes for ventilation. Jeff Kask, Tyler Beard, and "Stoney" Wellman show some of their favorites, *right: above, left to right,* and *below, right to left.* Most cowboys own at least two hats—one for work and one for dress.

FANCY DUDS

Buffalo Bill, Western movies, and dude ranching did more for cowboy fashion than the cowboys of old ever did. Working cowboys hardly had money enough to clothe themselves, and their garments were an assortment of ill-fitting pants and shirts that had no discernible style. Sturdy, long-wear blue jeans, invented for the rough Forty-niners by the Levi-Strauss Company of San Francisco, were adopted by many working men in the

Teresa and Tyler Beard's cowboy collection includes beautifully decorated shirts, such as this Ride 'em Cowboy shirt hanging on an old cupboard, *opposite.* Fancy floral motifs such as on the back of the shirt modeled by Teresa Beard, *above,* are especially popular and match the motifs of the carved floral decoration on leather belts, saddles, and boots, as can be seen in the shirt and boots from the collection of Jack Pressler, who models them at his home in Santa Fe, *right.*

West. Shirts were durable and were made from coarse fibers. Buffalo Bill, the first to introduce the cowboy into show business through his Wild West Show in the 1880s, was also the first to adopt a particular look for himself and his actor-cowboys. With the cowboy as entertainer—showing off his skills in rodeos and on stage—fancy Western shirts and crisply ironed jeans began to appear. Dudes raised the cowboy look to new heights, with fashions developed back East for their sojourns out West. The basic wardrobe of the properly attired dude consists of stylish vests, shirts with appliquéd cowboy motifs, "Peewee" (short) boots, and, of course, the bolo tie. No one knows exactly how the bolo came to be invented, but it has maintained steady popularity in the West; it is the official neckwear, formal and informal, of both Arizona and New Mexico. Navajo- and Zuni-made bolos are especially coveted.

Roger Miller of Glorieta, New Mexico, has made bolos based upon 19th-century artist Charlie Russell's vision of the cowboy, *opposite,* and Jerry Valdez, *right,* of Great Falls, Montana, has taken the fancy engraved scrollwork of cowboy silver and used it to decorate his bolo ties.

SADDLE LEATHER

The saddle has been a part of riding since medieval times, but the rigors of the New World created a need for adaptations to its design. From the merger of the medieval war saddle and the racing saddle common to the Moslems came a new Mexican-styled stock saddle that was designed to accommodate the *vaquero*, who spent long hours in the saddle and who also had to be prepared to ride hard and fast when the herd was on the move. Heavy but not too heavy, a Western saddle provides some protection for the rider, is easy to mount and dismount, and can be ridden for many hours at a stretch. Its horn helps keep the rider seated and holds the most important tool of his trade—the rope. While the form of the saddle remained essentially the same, stirrups, skirts, and forks varied from region to region. The saddle a man rode and the manner in which he roped identified his place of origin.

The "Complete Cowboy" is seen here in a historic photograph from the collection of Teresa and Tyler Beard, *left.* The magnificent saddle and wild and woolly chaps must have been the pride of this young man posing with his finest possessions. Saddle maker Jeff Kask, *opposite,* enjoys the New Mexican sun with his faithful dog. Beside him are a few samples of his handiwork. Kask began working on saddles out of frustration with gear then available. Retired cowboys often pursue one of the skills or talents they developed on the range, when they leave the hard cowboy life— often as early as their thirties.

A saddle collection, *opposite,* gives a hint of the variety of forms that the Western stock saddles took from year to year and from region to region. The high horns and cantles helped to keep the rider seated and broad skirts on the saddles protected both horse and rider. A saddle made by Jeff Kask, *right,* shows in detail the type of leather tooling and silver ornamentation that makes a fine saddle a work of art. As one of the most valuable tools owned by a horseman, the saddle is a source of great pride.

FORGING THE OLD WEST

In the Old West, work on the ranch and in the larger community would quickly have ground to a halt without the blacksmith. Iron, among the earth's most abundant resources, was absolutely essential to almost every aspect of ranch life. The wagons that carried settlers westward also carried anvils, hammers, and tongs, and few groups would have been so foolhardy as to travel without a blacksmith to keep the wagons rolling. When Cortés arrived on the shores of

Horseshoes come in nearly as many sizes and styles as men's shoes. Not just horses, but oxen and mules wore shoes, each fashioned to size by the smith, *above left.* Ranches often had more than one brand, and cattle were marked to indicate their status on the ranch when they were ready for market. The blacksmith also provided the tools for the rancher at branding time, *left.*

Mexico in 1519, he brought with him three blacksmiths. Before the Spanish, the New World had no iron working, although native groups were known to work in copper, tin, silver, and gold. Throughout the colonial era in the West, iron shortage was a serious problem, since miners preferred to extract the abundant and more lucrative silver. All of the farm implements, wagon fittings, branding irons, chains and hooks, horseshoes, bits and spurs, mining gear, builder's hardware, and even household tools such as spoons depended upon the services of those who worked in iron. A big ranch such as the Grant-Kohrs in Deer Lodge, Montana, would have had a blacksmith on hand at all times to keep the ranch running.

A lady smith works at the anvil and forge on the Grant-Kohrs Ranch to show visitors the many skills of the blacksmith, *left.* **Behind her a rack of horseshoes in standard sizes and shapes are ready to be custom-fitted to the individual animal.**

TRUE WESTERNERS

The house was the oldest in Comanche, Texas, and it was also the most dilapidated, when Teresa and Tyler Beard decided it was time to come to the rescue. Saved from the bulldozer, the old Texas home became part of their consuming passion for collecting Western memorabilia. After years in other parts of the country and in Europe, the Beards came home to Texas with the enthusiasm of true lovers of their state and all that it represents. Tyler's great uncle, a Texas Ranger at the turn of the century, inspired Tyler's devotion to gathering and preserving his Western collection. The couple are forever searching for the best boots, Texas furniture, photographs, and Western wear. Although they sell some cowboy gear, there have always been things that they just couldn't bear to part with—their home pays homage to these favorite objects.

The beautiful stone home of Teresa and Tyler Beard, *opposite*, was once in ruins; only their determination and hard work brought it back to life. The modest proportions are typical of early Texas homes. Large windows provided ventilation during the hot summer months; the stone walls kept the home well insulated against temperature extremes. *Below*, Teresa and Tyler Beard stand before another vintage item in this collection—their pickup truck. No Texas ranger would be without his faithful pickup.

Vintage photographs stand before ancient wooden shutters in the Beard home, *above.* The living room, *right,* has a rustic flavor enhanced by the stone walls and unfinished pine furnishings. Pendleton blankets add a bit of color to the warmth of the pine furniture and woodwork. On the wall a Navajo rug provides a bold statement in red.

The dining room is set for the perfect cowboy meal, with plates bearing cowboy motifs and fringed leatherwork adorning one of the chairs. The Navajo rug over the chest in the background is in a pattern of crosses popular in the 1920s.

A simple cupboard displays a collection of cowboy china. Restaurant china manufacturers, such as the Wallace China Company, made heavy, durable china with cowboy motifs for the many Western restaurants and dude ranches. Today, such restaurant china is highly valued by collectors.

Covering the big log bed that dominates the bedroom are fine examples of Pendelton blankets. In the corner a hat rack contains Tyler Beard's collection of cowboy hats. Above the bed, a vintage photograph shows a cowboy get-together. At the bedside rests a pair of fancy vintage boots.

BEST OF THE BOOTS

Not too long ago, cowboy boots were not a fashion statement but just another tool in a working man's wardrobe. Today's boots—lasted into high- and low-top models; with pointed, round, and square toes; made of every conceivable type and color of leather; and appliquéd and stitched with a multitude of fancy designs—can be found more often on the feet of those who have never been near a horse than they can on those of the cowboys for whom they were invented.

Some wags claim that the cowboy boot was designed to prevent cowboys from ever learning how to walk, but there are a few more practical reasons for its particular style. The high, heavy leather tops shield the legs against the constant dangers of the job; the deep-slung, high heel accommodates both stirrup and spur. Like the saddle, the boot became one of the few spots for embellishment in an otherwise plain world.

A fine collection of boots of all sizes and colors are displayed upon the shelves of a pine cupboard at the Texas home of Teresa and Tyler Beard, *left*. Highly ornamented boots became very popular during the 1950s, and were worn primarily on dress occasions. A fancy Lone Star spur is worn with an equally fancy pair of boots, *opposite*.

Before the turn of the century, men in all walks of life in the West wore boots. The high-topped boots of the cowboy sported a band around the top, which sometimes had some form of decoration such as a star. Bootstraps, which helped ease the tight-fitting footgear over trail-weary heels and toes, eventually grew into absurd "mule ear" straps, then later shrank to barely functional tabs. Spur leathers fit across the instep and added to the overall look of the boot. Scroll stitching remains the standard for fine boots, but many elaborations have varied the theme of this basic decoration. Rhinestone cowboys, movie stars, country Western singers, and rodeo stars have all contributed to the evolution of the cowboy boot into a fine art.

A collection of men's and women's boots on these pages is the pride of Jack Pressler of Santa Fe.

JINGLE JANGLE

Spanish colonists and soldiers might sport spurs with three- or four-inch rowels, or the massive *estribos de cruz*, weighty iron cross-shaped spurs, and they used them not only as horse prods but for show and protection. Like other features of the American cowboy's gear, Western spurs originated in Mexico and many were made there as well. Since they were primarily tools, spurs had little need of decoration, but some were nevertheless personalized with initials or other lettering, or engraved with symbols important to the owner, such as "gal legs" or card suite designs. Applying the ingenuity that comes from weeks on the trail, cowboys often fashioned spurs of their own design, relying on an old Ford axle for the metal and trial and error for the outcome.

A spur collection assembled by Dan and Judy Coates of Granbury, Texas, shows the whimsical decorative motifs that often appear on Texas spurs, *opposite.* "Gal legs" and stars, symbolic of the Lone Star State, are among the designs. Conchos, including conchos made from Mexican coins, decorate many spurs. Spurs at work, *above right* and *right,* adorn the boots of cowboys momentarily at rest. Initials and whole names are common to spurs and help to keep ownership of the gear out of contention.

FANCY BELTS/ TROPHY BUCKLES

The primary purpose of the belt may appear to be to hold up pants, but in the West, a belt exists to display a buckle. For cowboys, a buckle can be a significant piece of hardware, tantamount to jewelry. Trophy buckles are worn by those who hang onto bucking broncos, wrestle steer, rope calves, and ride bulls. For spectators, there are fancy buckles that imitate the flashy appeal of the trophies. Tom Paul Schneider of Gilbert, Arizona, casts and engraves trophy buckles and

Cast silver ornaments with horses, steers, and cacti were made by Roger Miller in Glorieta, New Mexico, *left.* Belts, as well as hatbands, sport silver ornaments at O'Farrell's Hat Company in Durango, California, *top right.* The beautifully tooled belts, *center right* and *right,* are made by Mariel Webb, at Caballo, Santa Fe.

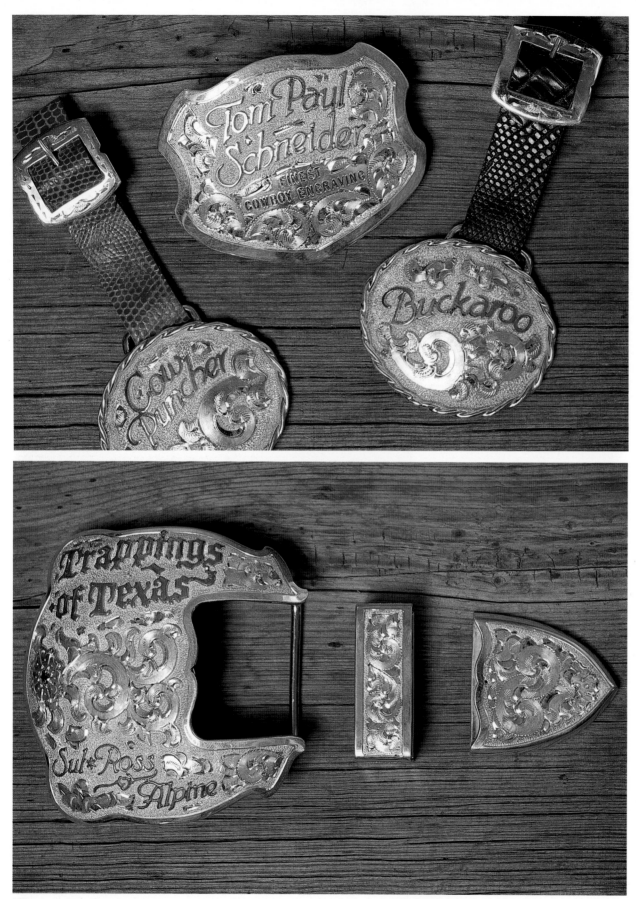

works the silver bits, spurs, bridle mounts, and other adornments for cowboy and horse. His meticulously hand-engraved scroll and floral designs mimic the engraved leather found on many fine saddles. Inlays of jewels and gold highlight the engraved patterns or outline the entire buckle.

Like Schneider, many engravers and jewelers start their careers by making functional metal hardware, then find that true satisfaction lies in the fine craftsmanship of the final decoration. Most are trained in the usual school of the West—the school of hard knocks—working with blacksmiths or on their own, gradually developing a distinctive style. Many work only part-time at their craft while devoting much of their time to ranching; almost all come to the craft from cowboying.

Tom Paul Schneider of Gilbert, Arizona, made the watch fobs and belt buckle, *above left* and *left*. Made for special events and occasions, trophy buckles are tangible evidence of the proficiency of their wearer. Jerry Valdez of Great Falls, Montana, makes special-order trophy buckles for clients all over the West, *opposite*.

COWBOYANA

It is to all the little buckaroos and buckarettes that we must owe thanks for the trivial objects of everyday life emblazoned with cowboy motifs. Without kids or commercialism there would be no Hopalong Cassidy wristwatches or Roy Rogers bedspreads. The popularity of Western movies by the 1930s opened the way; soon cereals and spiral notebooks appeared with images of favorite movie and radio heroes. They all projected an image of upright role models: Gene Autry stood by his Cowboy Commandments, and Hopalong Cassidy ordered only straight root beer. Once TV dominated every living room, cowboys were there too; first and foremost Buffalo Bob and his marionette companion, Howdy Doody. As baby boomers aged, cowboys took to smoking and drinking on screen, but the relics of the golden era of show business cowboys lingered on in souvenirs of every description.

From collar points to playing cards, any object with the cowboy motif, the wilder the better, is the consuming interest of Michael Collier of Phoenix, Arizona, *opposite*. Ed Mell's fine painting of a bucking bronc rider hangs over Collier's bed in a room crammed to brimming with cowboyana, *right*.

Phoenix collector Michael Collier's treasures include copper and brass cowboy hat ashtrays, enameled dinnerware with chuck wagon and brand motifs, and clocks, lamps, and nightlights, *left.* A great collection of all types of miniatures and other cowboy kitsch occupies the desk of a collector in Austin, Texas, *opposite.* Miniature boots and other trinkets were often made for the pleasure of youngsters enamored with the cowboy imagery so popular in the 1950s.

'steer-riding'
ANNUAL AMERICAN LEGIO
COWBOYS REUNION
LAS VEGAS, N.MEX.
AUG. 1-2-3

RODEO DAYS

The rodeo sums up the cowboy's skills, and then ventures off into the realm of thrill seeking and showing off. Events such as team roping, calf roping, saddle bronc riding, and bareback riding are a logical extension of the everyday tasks of a cowboy, but the origins of bullriding are a mystery, since there is no functional need to climb on the back of an angry bull. Like the *charrería*, the rodeo grew as a form of entertainment and competition among working cowboys, probably right on the ranch at first, then among several ranches, and later in town.

There are a number of claims to the site of the first rodeo in America. When Buffalo Bill hit the road with the Wild West Show in the 1880s, rodeos began to take their show business aspects more seriously, becoming more formal, more lucrative, and better organized. Events began to be timed and judges took style as well as stamina into account in the competition. Professional associations came into being. As the life of the cowboy changed, maintaining a standard for what constituted a real cowboy assumed a new importance.

At the Las Vegas, New Mexico, rodeo in the 1940s, bystanders and cowboys crowded the area for a good look, *above left.* At the Tucson rodeo, bullriding was, in the 1960s, *left,* and remains today, *opposite,* a popular and dangerous event. Scenes from the Tucson rodeo, *following pages,* illustrate the excitement of the event.

CHAPS

There are Texas legs and Batwings, good old Cheyenne legs and the outrageous Woolies, but nothing beats the new gaudy rodeo colors for true snappy chappies. Chaps remain an important utilitarian piece of gear for the working cowboy and a great means of self-expression for competitors at rodeo time. Chaps, like Western spurs and hats, owe their origins to the Mexican *vaquero*, whose *chaparreas* were leather breeches worn over pants to safeguard the rider's legs from the dense spiky vegetation that always seemed to attract wild cattle. To give the rider maximum comfort and maneuverability in the saddle, chaps cover only the legs, not the seat. Modified to serve the varied terrain of the West, chaps took on different styles, studded with silver, fringed, and with and without pockets.

Of all cowboy gear, chaps are most likely to be made by the cowboy or his sweetheart. Simple in construction, chaps are tailored to fit the individual. Cowboys at work and rest, *opposite,* wear simple chaps fastened with conchos and rawhide. The turn-of-the-century cowboy, *right,* models a beaded and fringed leather shirt and fringed pants that were probably made by Native Americans.

FOAMING MUGS AND SWINGING DOORS

Like the golden era of cowboying, the period of the true saloon, as depicted in countless Westerns, was short-lived. Most saloons in the West lacked the amenities of mahogany bars, gilt-framed mirrors, and pretty women. Rather, they were rough and crude beer halls where men congregated to drink themselves senseless. The drink of choice was very strong whiskey of the moonshine variety, probably greater than 100 proof, sold under such apt brand names as Taos Lightning. Saloons offered the op-

A barful of customers came out to the street to immortalize and celebrate the virtues of beer in this late 19th-century New Mexican photograph, *left.* Men at pleasure in the Arizona Territory, Tucson, in 1903, have an elegant bar as a backdrop, *top right.* German brewers made life a bit easier in the Far West with the introduction of fine brews such as those served in this Albuquerque establishment about 1885, *center right.* The rough aspect of frontier Montana is evident in this scene, *right,* with the fiddler and the ladies of the establishment lined up with the customers of a hard-drinking saloon.

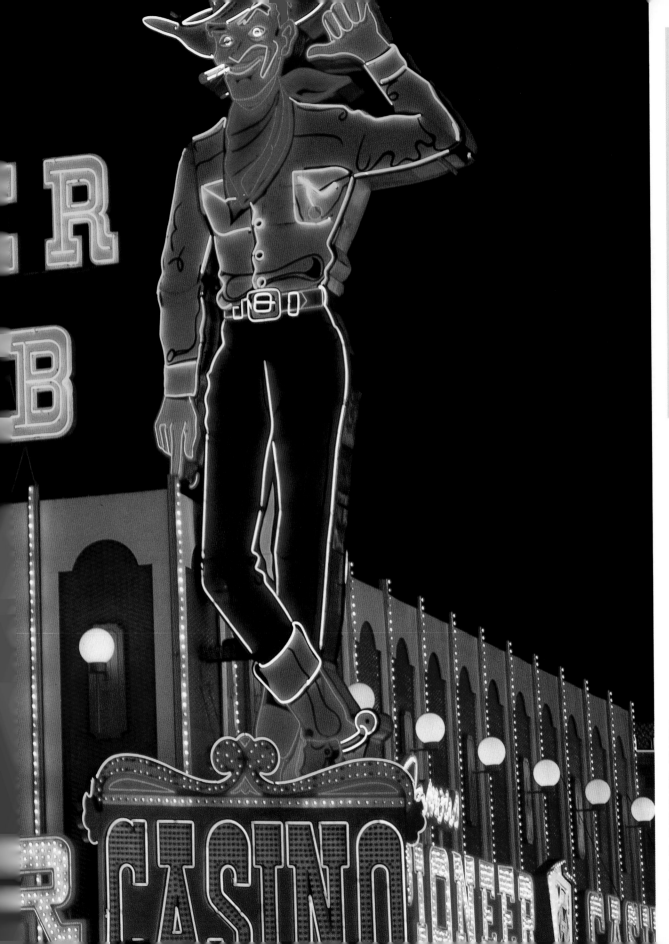

portunity not only to go blind but also to be killed. Brawls and gunfights at close quarters reflected the general state of chaos that characterized the wilder establishments. The only women permitted beyond the swinging doors were on hand to encourage the consumption of alcohol. Gambling was a popular form of entertainment at the saloon, and professional gamblers, better dressed and wealthier than farmers and ranch hands, were often regarded as the aristocrats of the West. As life became less reckless on the Western frontier, saloons grew more sedate, becoming eating and entertainment centers. Prohibition finally laid to rest saloon life as it was known during the last half of the 19th century.

Las Vegas, the center for gambling in today's West, pays its respects to its roots in the Old West, as in this giant neon cowboy, *left.* Other famous watering holes from throughout the West—including Sheridan and Jackson Hole, Wyoming—continue to draw a steady stream of cowboy customers, *opposite.* The beer bottles, *opposite center right,* are on display at the Lone Star Brewery in San Antonio.

PEACE-MAKERS AND TROUBLE-MAKERS

Wars make the weapons, it is said, and this was certainly true of the weapons of the West. Until the Civil War, guns were cumbersome, difficult to load, and notoriously unreliable. Samuel Colt designed rapid-fire revolvers used during the war with Mexico in 1846, and his percussion military models were widely used during the Civil War. But it was the Colt Single Action .45 caliber—the so-called Peacemaker, evidently named without irony—that became the handgun most closely associated with the gunfighters and other frontier ways of the West. Gunfighting with the Colt .45

Studio portraits of cowboys, cowgirls, gunmen, and sheriffs represent the full-dress regalia of Western folks in the late 19th century, *opposite.* A pair of law officers, *right,* stare nervously into the camera and hold their lever action rifles in a most peculiar manner—perhaps at the instruction of an equally nervous photographer.

could be a hit-or-miss affair. The image promoted by television programs of the 1960s of gunfighters facing off at opposite ends of town had little basis in reality, since the revolver's effective range was about 75 feet and accuracy in the heat of battle was probably about 20 feet. Many fights were most likely at a range of 7 or 8 feet —not sporting enough even for television to reproduce. Although most men owned weapons few carried them, since they would interfere with the work routine. Also popular were the Bowie knife and the Winchester rifle.

Leather craftsman Jeff Kask, *left*, models the holster and vest he made for himself. Like most gun owners and makers of Western gear, Jeff has definite opinions about how gunmen once wore their pistols: his theory is that a gunman would have to cross over to extract a gun quickly. In Joe Gish's Old West Museum in Fredericksburg, Texas, a wall filled with guns, holsters, chaps, and other typical gear memorializes both lawmakers and outlaws, *opposite.*

A holster in the collection of Joe Gish, *opposite,* is tooled in an intricate basketweave design. Badges at Gish's Old West Museum, in Fredericksburg, Texas, once identified the local law as marshal, constable, or sheriff, *right.*

THE DUDE ARRIVES

Once the cowboy's nemesis, the dude—anyone who doesn't know what he's doing and when to do it—has rescued many a failing ranch over the years. Dude ranching often proved to be more lucrative than cattle ranching and became especially popular in the scenic regions of Colorado, Wyoming, and Montana.

The old dude ranches were basically landlocked cruise ships that offered a taste of the Old West. Some employed wranglers, who supervised all the activities at the corral and provided musical entertainment in the evenings. Sometimes working ranches also gave a few paying visitors a sense of cowboy life by allowing them to participate in round-ups, trail drives, and the upkeep of the ranch. Along with the popularity of the cowboy, dude ranching has waxed and waned, and waxed again.

Barlow's Ranch in the Sierra Verde of New Mexico, photographed around 1929, shows the merging of the automobile and the resort-style manor as well as wonderful uses of pine poles for the construction of buildings and fences, *left.* Dude ranches in Arizona in the 1950s were the forerunners of the large resorts that now predominate in that state, *top right.* A view from the porch of the Canjilon Ranch, about 1925, New Mexico, *center right,* and the Diamond J Ranch in Montana, *right,* show the classic dude experience.

PART THREE

HIGH ADVENTURE

DREAMS OF THE PIONEERS, EXPLORERS, AND MYTHMAKERS

The way west was paved not so much with *good* intentions as with *dogged* intentions. One way or another the pioneers, explorers, goldpanners, surveyors, businessmen, and mail-order brides were intent on getting ahead in life. And often the means of achieving success seemed to beckon from the western horizon. Regarded as a place of hope, the West was foremost a place of ambition.

The first wave of westward movement was a reconnoitering mission, carried out by the government in hopes of determining the scope of the West's geography and natural resources, and by businessmen, who sought the means and methods of exploiting those resources.

Mapping the West was no easy task, since it was immense, difficult to travel through, and cut off from communications. Some of the more effective explorers of the mountains and plains

Recreational fishing came early to the West. These gentlemen show off their catch on the banks of the White River, Colorado, about 1895.

were the fur trappers and traders, who succeeded in documenting much of the western territory but who also completely depleted the West of valuable fur-bearing animals in a few short decades. They also nearly succeeded in exterminating the American bison, the buffalo—a situation that rankled the Native Americans who depended upon the beast for their livelihood.

The story of the buffalo and its demise is in many ways the quintessential Western story: filling the Plains was once a magnificent animal—a seemingly unlimited resource. No governmental controls limited who could hunt, when, how, how many animals could be killed, or for what reason. So the buffalo were slaughtered in staggering numbers, primarily for the hides—slaughtered to the point of no return. When the Native Americans sought to preserve their traditional hunting territory, the U.S. Army arrived to establish forts for the distribution of the hides and the protection of the traders.

The West was the place of freedom—free land, free animals, free minerals, free forests, free grasslands—and there were those who sat down to this feast with wild abandon. As the frontier of exploitation receded, conflicts were inevitable in the competition for resources that were, in fact, finite. Lines were

forever being drawn between factions; often the winner was the owner of the biggest or most guns. Bringing the law to the West proved to be as problematic as introducing many other institutions. The shaping of the culture and economy of this vast area is sometimes referred to as the "winning of the West," as if it were a prize awarded for winning a great contest. If it was any type of a contest, it was one of endurance.

Just getting to the West was arduous. Many families who set out in the first wave of pioneering never arrived at their destination. The overland trails that started in Missouri crossed hundreds of miles of wilderness without benefit of communication or way station. The trails traversed high mountain passes, rushing rivers, and arid deserts, and crossed hostile territory. Those who went to farm lived on the margin: if their first crops failed, there was no bank to turn to for a loan, not even a poorhouse. Instead, early pioneers relied on each other for survival, aiding their neighbors in distress, fostering a sense of community, and developing independent means of governing themselves and resolving problems. Loyalty and charity became paramount values in the communities of the Old West.

Meanwhile, the West's entrepreneurs—those who went for minerals or timber or fur—usually met adversity utterly alone, without family or community for support. The West became the great leveler in American society: it belonged to the ambitious, the adventurer, and the risk taker, not to those who made their way by birthright or by following the rules.

Photographer Ben Wittick, who captured the people and places of the West, here poses for his own camera about 1882.

These first Westerners were repeating the experience of the earlier settlers of the Eastern colonies, fleeing from a rigidly stratified society to a place were they could make a society of their own. When they came, however, they usually came to stay. No sooner had a home or town been built than the process of change and improvement began. The simple, square log cabin was annexed in every direction. Sometimes upwardly mobile homeowners faced the logs with siding or simply erected a bigger, grander house nearby and turned the original homestead into one of many outbuildings. In towns, board sidewalks gave way to paving stones, and frame facades made way for granite. The train, the stage, and the freight wagons brought the goods of the manufacturing East to the pioneer West: new and better tools, luxuries such as mahogany furniture and pianos, books, china, and imported textiles. The need for home, stability, and family shaped westward expansion. If men came westward without a wife, they were forever in search of one. Though much has been made of the lawless and rough West, what was most sought after was a hearth and home. Communities clamored for communication and transportation, and in turn worked to make their town attractive, quickly building banks, schools, and churches so that other settlers would follow and join them.

Soldiers enjoy an impromptu meal at a fort in the Arizona territory, *above*. The Overland Coach of White Sulphur, Montana, pauses for a pose, *below*.

Establishing homes and communities was hard work and tough scrabble, but the West also meant a limitless horizon and the freedom to have fun. Westerners set about their pleasures with the same enthusiasm and energy that they brought to their work, and many of their pleasures could be described as extensions of work—chopping contests among loggers and drilling contests among miners. But the West's most enduring reward was its natural beauty. The national parks were born from the urge to preserve what everyone knew at heart was not limitless—the vast American wilderness. Uninhabited, unexploited space was the greatest resource that the West possessed.

Despite Man's relentless attempts to diminish Nature, Nature still triumphs in this part of America. When you drive from east to west across the continent, there comes a magic point when you realize that the sky has somehow changed, becoming an unobstructed and perfect hemisphere meeting the horizon in a neat, clear line. The sky is now immense: you have reached the West. People become almost insignificant as the sky and land dominate. Everything that is in nature becomes greater than everything that is without. Although giant dams, electric lines, and highways proclaim the cleverness of the species, the great outdoors is everything. The history of the West is a study in man's attempts to conquer, subdue, and develop the land. All along the way West there are notable failures in his overall success at doing so. The mountains still accumulate so much snow in the winter that they become impassable, the Plains still live in a cycle of water that no one can predict, and the desert continues to resist human inhabitation.

WAGONS WEST

Old trails and faint ruts are the only traces of the immense westward migration of people whose wagons, following animal and Indian tracks, wore their way into Western soil. The earliest trails went not just east to west but from south to north, up the Camino Real from Mexico to the farthest northern frontier of the Spanish empire. The first of the great east-west routes—the Old Santa Fe Trail—opened up the Spanish West, and its goods and people, to the East. Over the Oregon and California trails rolled the wagons of the pioneers. Confronting starvation, frostbite, and exhaustion during the several months it took to make the journey, they pushed and pulled their wagons along mountain passes, across rivers, and through the ancient territories of the Indians. By the mid-19th century, the stream of immigrants had become a deluge, as the Forty-niners covered the Overland Trail in their eagerness to reach the goldfields of California.

Despite their questionable utility in the 20th century, wagons and wagon wheels are saved and salvaged throughout the West as mementos of pioneer days. *Top left, top far left, left,* and *above far left,* wagons are preserved at the Ranching Heritage Center in Lubbock. A few reminders of the trek along the Santa Fe Trail remain at Fort Union, New Mexico, *far left* and *left.* The Tetons serve as backdrop for an abandoned buckboard in Jackson, Wyoming, *opposite.*

ROUGHING IT

The expansion of agriculture west of the Mississippi after the Civil War was the most extensive new cultivation of land ever undertaken. The Homestead Act of 1862 caused an explosion of settlement and farming in the West, and a new conflict between the cattlemen, who had enjoyed free use of grazing lands, and the farmers, who could claim (and fence off) 160 acres each from lands in the public domain. Settlements along the line of the railroad kept pushing back the frontier. Perhaps the most memorable event of homesteading was the opening up of parts of the Oklahoma Territo-

The true ambience of homesteading is captured in this 1883 photograph of Mormon settlers near Snowflake, Arizona, *opposite.* The roughness of the life, the importance of family, and the pride of achievement are all reflected in this family's portrait. In the sparsely populated West, animals were important to survival. The New Mexican ranch wife, about 1900, *above right,* clearly has affection for the family burro. Timber was an essential for homesteading: the tallest trees made the largest buildings, *right.*

ries in a "run" of land boomers
—later to be called "sooners"
—those who tried to sneak
onto the land before the official
opening date and who settled
the areas literally overnight.
Most homesteading, though,
was a protracted process involv-
ing years of clearing and developing land.

Settlers often had little more
than the land they had
claimed, and they came to de-
pend on mutual assistance and
their own abilities in construction, plant and animal hus-
bandry, and domestic skills.
Ingenious use of local resources, such as the sod for
houses on the Plains, saved
many a family during the hard
early years of settlement.

**Large areas of the West remain as
unpopulated today as they were a
hundred years ago. The vastness of
the space and the loneliness of the
work can be seen in this young
man's vigil, caretaking his flock. The
windmill is often the tallest structure
on the prairie—an essential feature
of a ranch or community that had no
surface source of water, *following
pages.***

The interior of a homesteader's dwelling at the historic museum setting in Winedale, Texas, *left*, consists of a few simple tools, a single table for food preparation, and a fireplace for warmth and cooking. A simple rectangular structure with pitched roof and front porch was the basic architectural style of Texas, often based on German prototypes. Johnson Settlement in Johnson City, Texas, is at right; other simple stone dwellings are below right and bottom right. With few moments of beauty in their daily routine, homesteaders welcomed the ebullient blooming of wildflowers in spring and summer, *following pages.*

A TOWN AT A TIME

Towns grew up where water, climate, and soil conditions were most favorable, and where there was the best access to transportation—by land or water. Once the railroad reached a town, the town's success was assured. Towns vied for the opportunity to become a stop on the rail line and ceded prime property to the railroads for their rights of way and stations.

The other force in the success of a community was the nature and vision of its inhabitants. Towns fortunate enough to have strong-minded and forward-thinking civic leaders often succeeded, while other towns attracted rough elements of society—lending a reputation that might color the perception of the community forever.

The townspeople of Thompson Falls, Montana, gathered on Main Street, the only street at this date, for a group portrait on July 2, 1889. The construction of a town often relied on the building of a sawmill to provide lumber. As time went on, brick storefronts gave the towns a more permanent look, as seen in many of the photographs of town buildings across the West, *following pages.*

LONE STAR STYLE

The young bride was the daughter of an old settler who had arrived in Texas in 1815, and the bridegroom was a native of the Carolinas lured to the free lands of Texas with his brother in 1831. Their new home was simply a big room with a loft above. But the Sam Lewis house, now part of the Winedale Historical Center in Round Top, Texas, grew as it passed from family to family, each one adding to its history, its size, or its decoration. Rudolph Melchior, a German artist, one of the many German-Americans to settle Texas, added stenciled and painted decorations to the walls and ceilings, giving the home a comfortable and somewhat elegant look. Like many early homes, the house achieved its present form without plan or design.

Also at Winedale, founded by the art collector Miss Ima Hogg as a repository of Texas history and design, is the McGregor home, a variation on the theme of a Southern plantation. Paint had to take the place of marble on mantels and also had to imitate other materials, yet the owners managed to bring a touch of their Southern home to the frontier.

The broad porches and open central hallway of the Sam Lewis house at Winedale were designed to mitigate the effects of the intense Texas summer, *opposite*. The view from the second-story porch of MacGregor-Grimm house at Winedale, *right*, shows the open country that once surrounded every Texas ranch.

On the porch of the Sam Lewis house a simple rocking horse was the pioneer child's first taste of the West, *left.* A doorway frames a view across the dogrun—the open central hallway—to the other side, *below left.* In the kitchen a cupboard holds the family china, *right.*

The interior of the MacGregor-Grimm house matches the exterior in frontier elegance. The parlor, *left*, shows a wonderful use of painted decoration on walls, ceilings, and mantel in lieu of the costly marbles, wallpapers, and other materials unobtainable on the Texas frontier. The dining room, *right* and a table in one of the bedrooms, *below right*, were not as elaborately decorated as the public parlor.

The West could not have been developed without the railroad. Cattle drives became obsolete once cattle could be loaded onto freight cars, as in the scene in Laguna Pueblo, New Mexico, about 1935, *far left.* Tourists first traveled upon the rails. The station at Silver City, New Mexico, about 1915–20 welcomed Americans from all regions and all levels of society, *left.* In Montana a railroad car, *below,* in 1895 served as a traveling exhibition for the territory, advertising free land as well as railroad owned land.

RIDING THE RAILS

May 10, 1869, stands out as one of the most important days in the history of the West. The golden spike driven into the earth at Promontory, Utah, where the Union Pacific and the Central Pacific railroads met, was an event that changed the face of the West. In 1865 the railroads could travel no farther west than Missouri; travelers could choose between a month to three months overland or many months by ship around the Horn. From 1865 to 1870 crews of Chinese and Irish immigrants laid over 20,000 miles of track in the West along a path that often closely paralleled old trails. After the railroad connected California to the East, the American continent became united, and the West was open to anyone with the price of a ticket. Americans could speed from coast to coast in a matter of days, even enjoying some luxuries during the trip. Pullman cars were the standard of comfort, with berths, dining cars, and even washrooms. The glass-domed observation car in the best-known transcontinental trains eventually came to epitomize luxury travel in the United States. Goods and people poured into the West, and Western products, particularly cattle, could now be shipped back to the East.

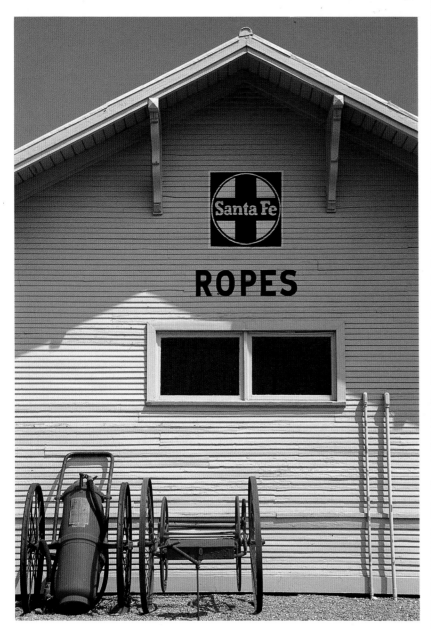

The historic station from Ropes, Texas, now stands at the Ranching Heritage Center in Lubbock, *above*. In its heyday, the station would have witnessed an active passage of traffic. A coal-filled potbelly stove kept passengers warm as they waited for the next train on pewlike benches or checked their weight for a penny, *right*.

MOUNTAIN MEN

Among the earliest explorers of the West were the trappers and fur traders who went in search of beaver, bear, raccoon, otter, and muskrat. For a brief time trappers had the West almost to themselves, plundering the immense wealth of its mountains and forests, and making the fortunes of a few companies and individuals, such as the Hudson's Bay Company and John Jacob Astor's American Fur Company. During the trapper's heyday, from about 1820 to 1840, these adventurers traveled freely along the waterways and mountains

At the annual rendezvous at the Martínez Hacienda in Taos, New Mexico, weekend mountain men gather to trade traditional wares. Taos was a historic trading center through the Spanish colonial period and during the heyday of the mountain men. At a convenient intermediate point between mountains and plains, Taos was a meeting place for the Spanish, Plains and Pueblo Indians, and trappers and traders.

of the West. At times large groups of men, as many as 100, would set themselves up in a region and work until it was virtually trapped out. Forts began to dot the landscape, serving as a point of supply and distribution for the trappers. The rendezvous was the idea of General William H. Ashley, who in 1825 reasoned that an annual meeting of trappers, traders, and Indians that moved from region to region would improve trade.

Each mountain man developed a singular costume. Clothed in leather, heavily bearded, with animal-fur headgear and the tools of his trade —knife and pistol—tucked into his belt, the trapper cut an immense figure in the American imagination.

Present-day mountain men follow the practice of the earlier trappers by making most of their clothing and gear. Fur hats and leather pants, as well as shirts of homespun and other simple handmade accoutrements, were typical of the men of the mountains, although few would sport a clean shirt.

Small leather beaded and fringed
bags once carried an adventurer's
tobacco and perhaps a little strike-
a-light, *left.* The ultimate trade good,
beads are still a perennial favorite of
the trade fairs, *above.* Made as far
away as Africa and imported through
Mexico, the beads were offered to
Native Americans in exchange for
furs and other valuables.

DIGGING DEEP

The gold panned out of Sutter's Mill, California, in 1849 was to be the first great strike in the West, and it inspired a mass migration. "Fortyniners" poured into California from every corner of the continent with pick, shovel and pan, rocker, and sluice. Thousands scoured the environs of Sutter's Mill—their desperation at never making a strike reflected in the wild behavior they displayed back in camp at the end of the day. Subsequent booms in Colorado and Nevada brought the same kind of seekers by the wagon load. Businesses and towns sprang up to meet the growing hordes, and much of the present-day character of the cities of Denver and San Francisco, not to mention that of the entire state of Nevada, can be attributed to the frenzy of the Gold Rush. The Comstock Lode of Nevada shifted the emphasis off gold and onto silver, but the results were similar. Land was populated and territories were created overnight.

A group of miners pose with the tools of their trade in Arizona, *left.* Prospectors set out to work from Tombstone, Arizona, *above right,* circa 1890s. The photographer Ben Wittick posed a group in Supa Canyon, Arizona, at the Coconina Silver Mine for *Struck It Rich, right.*

LOG CABIN HOME

The sturdy log cabin is the pioneer dwelling of America. Where lumber was available, the log cabin was the coziest and best home that could be erected with local materials. Although there were many methods of constructing a log home, the basic structural element was the notching at the four corners, which bore the load of the building. Simple saddle notching was common, but more elaborate dovetails and V-notched corners added considerably to the soundness of the structure. The timbers were often left rounded on the earliest dwellings, built in the haste of immediate need, then later hewn. A square, rough, or half-hewn timber made the interior more comfortable, easier to clad with siding and simpler to chink. Chinking of mud, stones, grass, or straw filled the cracks between the logs, keeping out wind, rain, and cold. Floor plans and construction varied according to which part of the country or from which country the pioneer hailed.

Out West, the wood of choice was pine. In areas where large pines were available, the buildings could be quite adequate, restricted only by the weight of the logs and the taper of the tree. Lodgepole pine, so-called because Plains Indians used it to make the poles for their tipis, was particularly desirable since it was so straight

A true tour de force of log house building was this lodge with multiple stories, porches, and wings at Brannin Ranch in Montana, *left.* An overland stage stops in front of the rustic log dwelling built in the Montana Territory, 1887, *above.*

and narrow. Lodgepole also became a popular wood for rustic chairs, tables, and beds.

It is hard to imagine a West in which timber did not play a major role. Not only was lumber the source of shelter for the early pioneer, but logging was often the industry that brought him to the West in the first place. It also made possible efficient mining, since lumber was needed to construct shafts for access to the deepest veins of ore. Railroads required great quantities of lumber for both fuel and railbeds. And without lumber, fencing, the aid of rancher and farmer, would not have been available. Lumbermen, like the cowboy, became legendary, another example of America's need to romanticize the frontier.

Like Montana, Wyoming favors the use of undressed and unpainted logs for many of its buildings, such as this series of cabins, guest houses, and barns from around the Jackson area, *left*. Old motel cabins can make great guest houses for when the children come to visit, *opposite*.

Exposed log walls at Owl Ranch in Wyoming create a warm setting for well-loved antiques and other treasures, *opposite.* Lodgepole pine has many applications for furniture, such as this simple straight-backed chair, *below,* and the bed and other furnishings in this bedroom at Owl Ranch, *right.*

ARTFUL HOMESTEAD

When you settle into the Rubbersnake Ranch in northern Wyoming with Bill and Barbara Schenck, you can expect to experience the conviviality and wit of the Old West and the owners' energy and enthusiasm for all things Western. Both artists, the Schencks work on several projects at a time, from painting huge canvases of pop cowboy imagery, tracking down lodgepole furniture, reconstructing prehistoric Indian pottery, keeping the library up to date, and adding on to the house and studio. Historic lodgepole furniture, pole-trimmed furniture, and massive pieces of burlwood make up the furnishings of the Rubbersnake Ranch, along with textiles with Western motifs and early Western paintings.

Rubbersnake Ranch is built for relaxing, enjoying the company of good friends, taking in the great outdoors, and cultivating a sense of appreciation for traditional Western arts.

In the dining room are Gila and Tanto pots, paintings by E. Irving Couse and William Leigh, and Bob Wade's retouched photograph called *Frontier Days, South Dakota, 1922, left.* According to its license plate Bill's pink Caddy is Too Cool, *below.*

Rubbersnake Ranch near Moran, Wyoming, *inset opposite,* is a summer home for Bill and Barbara Schenck and their collection of Pueblo pottery and Western historic paintings, *left.*

Upstairs at the Rubbersnake, a fortuitous find of a complete set of twigwork furniture from Sealy Lake, Montana, including a dresser, *above*, and bed and rocker, *right*, furnishes the master bedroom. A vintage bedspread and Navajo rug complete the room, along with a lamp shade made from photographic images of Schenck's paintings.

210

COLORFUL MEMORIES

From the turn of the century through the 1950s, beds in nearly every Western household were covered with the simple cotton blankets from Beacon Mills in Swannanoa, North Carolina. Started in the 1920s, Beacon made blended blankets often using Indian and cowboy motifs, but also featuring prosaic geometrics and florals. Woven in soft pastels or strong paintbox colors, they adorned many a twin bed in a child's bedroom. Special favorites of the 1950s were those with standard Indian motifs, such as bows and arrows or headdresses, and cowboy images—gunfighters and bronco breakers. Once ubiquitous, Beacon blankets spent several decades relegated to the back seat of the car, the dog's bed, or the summer cabin. As Western decor experiences a revival today, the Beacon blankets of happy childhood memories have returned to remind us of countless hours of "Gunsmoke," Buffalo Bob, Roy Rogers, and Hopalong Cassidy.

Well-worn Beacon blankets feature the popular geometric, pan-Indian as well as pictorial Western motifs. The age of the blankets is often revealed in the palette. These blankets probably date to the 1950s.

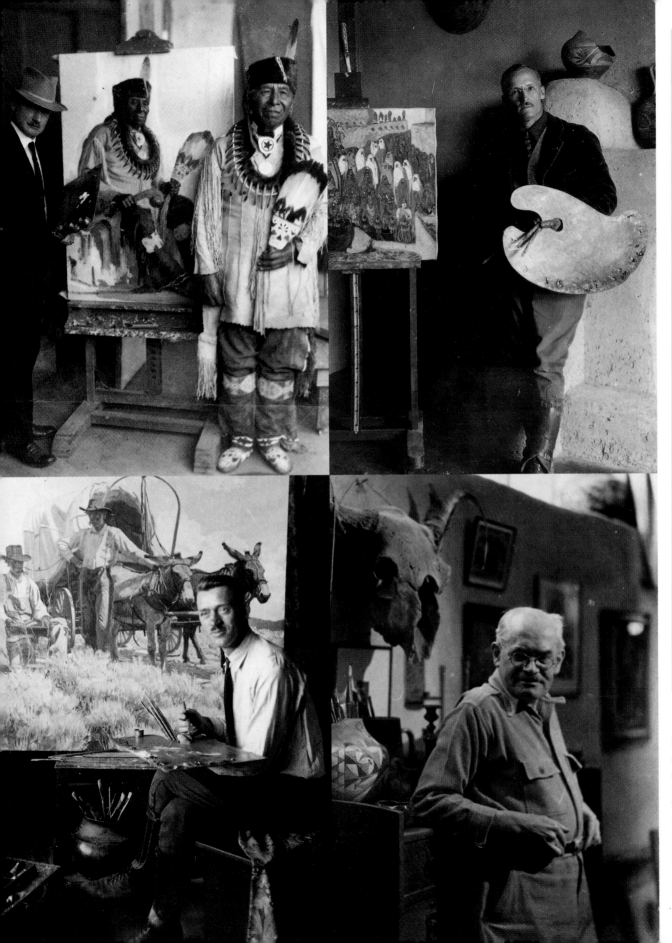

CAPTURING THE WEST

Arts and artists came to the West with the first settlers and sometimes long before. Serious pictorial studies of native life by George Catlin in the 1830s introduced the world to the behavior of indigenous people at the very moment these groups began to dwindle. The physical grandeur of the West was brought home through the overwhelming canvases of Albert Bierstadt and Thomas Moran in the late 19th century, which left an enduring impression of the immensity and intense beauty of the West. For Americans, and for many people around the world, the West became, even to those who might never see it, a romantic, awe-inspiring haven.

Surveyors, scientific expeditions, Army artists, and naturalists like John James Audubon also recorded the natural world. Native Americans contributed their own sensibilities and traditions to the developing pictorial richness of the West with Navajo blankets and Pueblo pottery—which in turn drew more and more artists to the West.

Santa Fe and Taos School painters are captured in their studios, surrounded by the objects of regional ethnographic interest that they often included in their paintings: *clockwise from top left,* **Henry Balink with the son of Sitting Bull; Ernest L. Blumenschein in his Taos home; Walter Ufer; and E. Martin Hennings. Joseph Imhot,** *opposite,* **works at Taos Pueblo.**

MYTHS OF THE GOLDEN WEST

There has been no greater merging of an American folk hero and commercialism than in the image of the cowboy. The need to sensationalize the cowboy began with the earliest publications and exhibitions of his image. Wild West shows presented a ruggedly handsome, fabulously dressed, athletic man who seemed to have absolute control over all large animals. Cheap dime novels expanded the tale by recounting godlike acts of daring and justice against rotten foes, and cowboy films quickly became a staple of the enterprise. Singing cowboys helped make the transition from the silent films to the talkies a smooth one, and the exuberant action and simple stories made the genre an early television choice as well.

Gone and forgotten stars of the West once signed hundreds of publicity photographs for avid fans. The "Singin' Cowboy," Jules V. Allen, *left,* had his moment of stardom in the 1940s.

A dreamy couple, Mary Beckwitt, dressed in an "Indian maiden" outfit including a great Pueblo Indian "squash blossom" necklace, and Bill West, in pure cowboy garb, *left,* pose in 1930. John Wayne, *above,* quickly became the premier cowboy star of feature films in the 1940s and 1950s, through a series of classic Westerns such as *Red River* and *Stagecoach.* The strong, silent image he perfected became the ideal of the cowboy.

O. K. CORRAL

FEED & LIVERY STABLES

HORSES, MULES, BOUGHT, SOLD, & TRADED

HAY & GRAIN. HORSE SHOEING. BLACKSMITH WORK

MULE & OX SHOES
MADE TO ORDER.

John Montgomery owner
1881

A large part of the appeal of the cowboy myth was the fact that he existed somewhere outside the tight confines of society. His freedom of action found a deep resonance among Americans, whose national sense of identity is so closely tied to individual rights. When the freedom-loving cowboy came into the civilized town, trouble was sure to follow—the plot for countless melodramas—for the town had law and order, women, saloons, gamblers, money, store-bought goods and any number of other temptations, authority figures, and evils. Beyond the reach of the town was salvation in the frontier. Although the frontier has undisputedly vanished, and the ranch and cattle industry faces economic hardships and opposition from environmental groups, affection for cowboy imagery continues to be strong.

Some Western towns that were all but forgotten came to life as tourist spots through the popularity of movie reenactments of historic events, such as the shoot-out at the O.K. Corral in Tombstone, Arizona. Visitors to Old Tucson, like Christine Mather, *above,* can be photographed in a favorite fantasy.

A street scene in Old Tucson, *left*, functions both as a movie set and as a tourist attraction. *Below left*, actors who reenact shoot-outs for visitors wait for the next show. *Below*, a cactus and a barber's pole are stereotypical images of the movie version of the West.

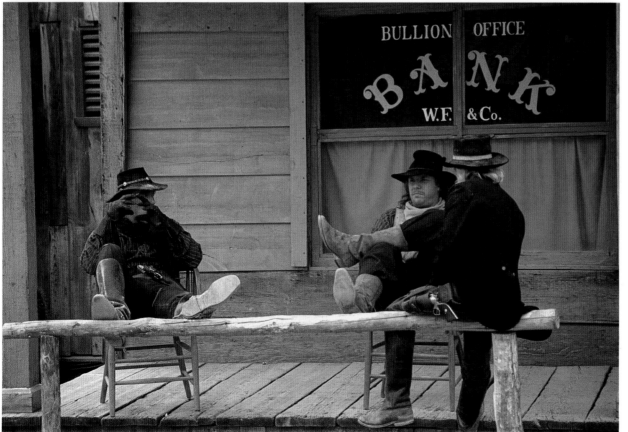

Western towns created especially for the movies strive for authenticity with their simple board sidewalks and frame buildings, such as at Old Tucson, *above.* Reproduction of vintage advertisements and notices are done in the bold typography typical of the period, then weathered for an Old West look, *right.*

THE END OF THE TRAIL

Along the trails and roads of the West many things have been left behind. Some of these are as ephemeral as youth, hope, and ambition; others are as concrete as gas pumps, log homes, and pickup trucks. The West is strewn with grandiose plans and poorly devised strategies, with hopes of getting rich quick, finding a place in the sun, and all the other myths of expansion that constitute so much of the American character. Since the 1890s, the American dream seems to have been defined by the boundless energy and enthusiasm symbolized by the Western frontier. The frontier vanished a mere 50 years after the West was opened up, but we retain a belief that somewhere on the Western horizon is a place that will fulfill all our dreams: "As long as there's a sunset, there will always be a West."

Rusting vehicles, *left,* and forgotten mom-and-pop operations such as motels, *below,* and gas stations and tourist camps, *following pages,* litter the Western byways as change and the restless forces of development continually alter the natural and human geography.

No matter where you go in the West, the legendary Western elements are slipping back to the earth. Fading away into the elements, the bones of an old truck are made insignificant by the more eternal image of the Tetons beyond, *right*. Outside Flagstaff, two gas pump sentries stand guard over a faded memory of a small business gone bust, *above*.

DIRECTORY

COLLECTING THE WEST

ARIZONA

Bacon's Boots and Saddles
290 North Broad Street
Globe, AZ 85501
(602) 425-2681
A Western store and saddle shop with handmade leather goods and a line of tailored Western clothing.

Collier Gallery
3632 North Bishop Lane
Scottsdale, AZ 85251
(602) 947-2787
This gallery organizes an energetic annual cowboy show.

Harry Thurston Saddlemaker
3144 East Bell Road
Phoenix, AZ 85032
(602) 992-4414
An internationally known saddle maker.

John and Bonney Herron Saddle and Boot Makers
Herron's Cowboy Shop
P.O. Box 1207
Chino Valley, AZ 86323
(602) 636-5461
Custom orders especially for the working cowboy.

John C. Hill
6990 East Main Street
Suite 201
Scottsdale, AZ 85251
(602) 946-2910
American folk and Indian arts.

Old West Outfitters
14255 North 79th Street,
Suite 6
Scottsdale, AZ 85260
(602) 951-9022
Authentic Western wear replicating that owned and made by the cowboys of the 1880s.

Paul Bond Western Boot Company
1065 Mariposa Road
Nogales, AZ 85621
(602) 287-3322
(602) 281-0512
One of the best-known custom bootmakers in America.

Que Pasa
7051 Fifth Avenue, Suite D
Scottsdale, AZ 85251
(602) 990-7528
Southwestern furnishings, accessories, and interior design.

R. Lloyd David and Sons Custom Saddlemakers
3132 East Prince
Tucson, AZ 85716
(602) 323-2598
The finest in custom saddles, made by those who truly care.

Rocky's Custom Saddlery
120 East Park Avenue
Gilbert, AZ 85234
(602) 926-4137
Custom-made saddles and related tack.

Santa Cruz Chili and Spice Company
Box 177
Tumacacori, AZ 85640
(602) 398-2591
Chile products and spices from around the world.

Tom Paul Schneider
P.O. Box 975
Gilbert, AZ 85234-0975
(602) 988-2005
Beautiful custom trophy buckles and saddle silver.

Stewart Boots
30 West 28th Street
South Tucson, AZ 85713
(602) 622-2706
Boots are fully handmade of 100 percent leather.

Superstition Mountain Supply Company
100 West Apache Trail, #110
Apache Junction, AZ 85220
(800) 541-0355
Supplies include fine handcrafted silver-mounted spurs.

Trophy Rope Company
18127 West Waddell Road
Waddell, AZ 85355
(602) 584-9489
Calf ropes in all sizes and strengths.

Yippie-ei-o!
4200 North Marshall Way
Scottsdale, AZ 85251
(602) 423-5027
Cowboy collectibles and interior design services.

CALIFORNIA

Federico
1522 Montana Avenue
Santa Monica, CA 90403
(213) 458-4134
Great Western stuff, Native American and Southwestern, and colonial Mexican jewelry and furniture.

Hemisphere
1426 Montana Avenue
Santa Monica, CA 90403
(213) 458-6853
Early California and Western items, ranch furniture, folk art.

High Noon
9929 Venice Boulevard
Los Angeles, CA 90034
(213) 202-9010
Belts, buckles, bolos, and horsehair items.

Historia Antiques
(by appointment)
Santa Monica, CA 90403
(213) 399-5152
South American, Spanish colonial, and 19th-century antiques.

Hollywood South West
4918 Vineland Avenue
North Hollywood, CA 91601
(818) 753-9050
Mexican and Navajo textiles, concho belts, and other Western jewelry.

Nonesuch Gallery
1211 Montana Avenue
Santa Monica, CA 90403
(213) 458-3773
Cowboy relics, Southwest Americana, and American Indian artifacts.

Sonrisa
8214 Melrose Avenue
Los Angeles, CA 90046
(213) 651-1090
Mexican folk art and Los Angeles Chicano art.

Umbrello
8607 Melrose Avenue
Los Angeles, CA 90067
(213) 659-4335
Mexican colonial furniture, antique Southwestern objects, as well as special lines of lamps, pottery, jewelry, and textiles.

COLORADO

Alex Pappas Cowboys Horsehair Company
302 Country Road 314
Ignacio, CO 81137
(303) 563-4387
Custom horsegear made using horsehair hitching.

Tony Baratono
814 Old Dutch Mill Road
Colorado Springs, CO 80907
(719) 599-3442
Collector, trader, seller, and buyer of Western memorabilia.

Bit, Spur and Saddle
National Collector's
Association
P.O. Box 3098
Colorado Springs, CO 80904
(719) 473-7101
An association that provides a newsletter with information on shows and auctions.

Crybaby Ranch
80 South Broadway
Denver, CO 80209
(303) 670-0773
An extensive collection of 1950s cowboy furniture, textiles, and jewelry.

Joan Roby Gallery
939 Broadway
Denver, CO 80203
(303) 892-9600
Western-style furniture and decorative arts.

Nan and David Pirnack Antiques
Willow Springs Center
2777 Iris
Boulder, CO 80304
(303) 444-6090
Unusual painted and Western furniture and folk arts.

Rusty May Saddlery
6239 West Highway 34
Loveland, CO 80538
(303) 663-4036
Custom saddles for all types of riders, including the handicapped.

Soda Creek Industries
Box 4343
Steamboat Springs, CO 80477
(800) 824-8426
(303) 879-3146
Western wear, dusters, and hats.

CONNECTICUT

J. Seitz and Company
Main Street, Route 45
New Preston, CT 06777
(203) 868-0119
Antiques and home accessories inspired by the spirit of the American Southwest.

DISTRICT OF COLUMBIA

The Phoenix
1514 Wisconsin Avenue N.W.
Washington, D.C. 20007
(202) 338-4404
Mexican crafts, jewelry, furniture, and folk art.

MONTANA

Archer's Grizzly Boot Company
814 South Higgins Avenue
Missoula, MT 59801
(406) 549-1555
Custom boots.

Bridger Creek Outfitters
P.O. Box 3576
Bozeman, MT 59715
(406) 586-7764
Outdoor clothing including slickers and handmade boots.

Gray Bear Horsehair Products
P.O. Box 487
Belgrade, MT 59714
(406) 585-4002
Quality hitched horsehair items made by Jeff Sailors.

Made Out West
P.O. Box 4087
Missoula, MT 59806
(406) 728-5520
Western goods such as hats, belts, bison jerky, and jewelry.

Montana Carriage Company
7457 Highway 2 East
P.O. Box 158
Columbia Falls, MT 59912
(406) 892-3133
Builders of horse-drawn vehicles.

Valdez Silversmiths
308 4th Avenue South
Great Falls, MT 59405
(406) 454-1211
Craftsmen of gold and silver cowboy and rodeo jewelry.

NEVADA

Jim Robertson's Buckaroo Sales
P.O. Box 60835
Las Vegas, NV 89160-0835
(800) 443-0564
(702) 735-4364
Many buckaroo items, including buckaroo suspenders and custom-made saddles.

William Stuart
P.O. Box 71207
Reno, NV 89570
(702) 852-7135
Buckaroo lace-up boots.

Tip's Western Wear and Custom Saddles
185 Melarkey Street
Winnemucca, NV 89445
(702) 623-3300
Bedrolls, sleeping bag covers, and other Western supplies.

NEW MEXICO

Andrew Smith Gallery
76 East San Francisco
Santa Fe, NM 87501
(505) 984-1234
Photographs of 19th- and 20th-century American West.

Beasly Trading Company
113 East Main
Farmington, NM 87401
(505) 327-5580
Long-time dealers in Navajo country arts.

Caballo
830 Canyon Road
Santa Fe, NM 87501
(505) 984-0971
Custom leather goods including tooled belts.

Marie Romero Cash
P.O. Box 1002
Santa Fe, NM 87504
(505) 983-1275
Maker of traditional Spanish New Mexican saint figures.

Claiborne Gallery
558 Canyon Road
Santa Fe, NM 87501
(505) 982-8019
Mexican colonial furniture.

Davis Mather Folk Art Gallery
141 Lincoln Avenue
Santa Fe, NM 87501
(505) 983-1660
(505) 988-1218
New Mexican animal woodcarvings, Mexican folk art, Navajo pictorial rugs, and other unpredictable arts.

Dwellings Revisited
Bent Street, P.O. Box 470
Taos, NM 87571
(505) 758-3377
Primitive northern New Mexican antiques from the turn of the century to the 1950s.

Bill Hawn
P.O. Box 8750
Santa Fe, NM 87504-8750
(505) 982-0202
Old cowboy gear, Native American and Western folk arts.

Horse Feathers, Etc.
P.O. Box 698
Ranchos de Taos, NM 87557
(505) 758-7457
Specializing in a good time with cowboy and Western stuff.

Horton's Saddle Shop
Box 73
San Jon, NM 88434
(505) 576-2482
Saddles made and repaired.

Jackalope Pottery
2820 Cerrillos Road
Santa Fe, NM 87501
(505) 471-8539
Folk arts and furniture, especially from around Latin America.

Lo Fino
The Dunn House Complex
Bent Street
Taos, NM 87571
(505) 758-0298
Southwestern furniture.

Roger Miller
Route 1, Box 3
Glorietta, NM 87535
(505) 757-6968
Sterling silver jewelry—bolos, belts, and earrings—inspired by Charlie Russell.

Montez Gallery
125 East Palace Avenue
Suite 33
Santa Fe, NM 87501
(505) 982-1828
Traditional Hispanic New Mexican art.

Mountain High Herb Company
Box L
Taos, NM 87571-0599
(505) 758-4144
Offer ancient New World products like blue corn.

Jack Pressler
920 Don Juan
Santa Fe, NM 87501
(505) 983-3547

Cowboy material including vintage boots and jewelry.

Old Southwest Trading Company
P.O. Box 7545
Dept. C-1
Albuquerque, NM 87194
(505) 836-0168
The chile aficionado's mail-order headquarters.

Rancho
322 McKenzie Street
Santa Fe, NM 87501
(505) 986-1688
Tradition and romance of the American West featured through legendary collectibles and home furnishings.

Richard Worthen Galleries
1331 Tijeras Street N.W.
Albuquerque, NM 87102
(505) 764-9595
An extensive collection of Spanish colonial antiques.

Roswell Seed Company
115-117 South Main
Roswell, NM 88201
(505) 622-7701
A wide variety of seeds including chile.

Bonifacio Sandoval
7222 Vivian Street N.E.
Albuquerque, NM 87109
(505) 821-4476
Tinwork mirrors, frames, sconces, and nichos.

Seth Gallery
1121B Paseo de Peralta
Santa Fe, NM 87501
(505) 988-7349
Traditional Southwestern art including the work of Hispanic weaver Teresa Archuleta Sagel.

Spider Woman Designs
225 Canyon Road
Santa Fe, NM 87501
(505) 984-0136
Chris O'Connell's weaving and design studio, focusing on the look of the Old West and Old Mexico with furniture, textiles, and decorative accessories.

Streets of Taos
200 Canyon Road
Santa Fe, NM 87501
(505) 983-8268
(505) 983-4509
Navajo rugs and jewelry, Spanish New Mexican 1930s furniture, calfskin lampshades.

Luis Tapia
Route 6, Box 01
Santa Fe, NM 87501

Maker of traditional Hispanic New Mexican folk art and furniture.

Textile Arts
Mary Hunt Kahlenberg
1571 Upper Canyon Road
Santa Fe, NM 87501
(505) 983-9780
Museum-quality textiles from around the world but especially the American West.

Wagon Mound Ranch Supply
P.O. Box 218
Route 271
Wagon Mound, NM 87752
(505) 666-2489
(800) 526-0482
A catalogue of tack, blacksmithing supplies, and packing equipment. Tons of horseshoes, all types.

Western Metal Arts
The Welchs'
Box 795
Tatum, NM 88267
(505) 398-5295
Maker of "silhouette"-style ranch signs.

Wolf Wagon Works
P.O. Box 927
Crossroads, NM 88114
(505) 675-2480
Specializing in rebuilding chuckwagons, buggies, and other horse-drawn vehicles.

NEW YORK

American Primitive Gallery
596 Broadway
New York, NY 10012
(212) 966-1530
Primitive and contemporary folk arts.

Pecos Valley Spice Company
500 East 77th Street
Suite 2324
New York, NY 10162
(212) 628-5374
Chile powder and gift items from the Southwest.

OKLAHOMA

G. C. Blucher Boot Company
350 North Main
Fairfax, OK 74637
(918) 642-3205
Started in 1915, this custom boot shop has made boots for John Wayne, Tom Mix, and John Ford.

TEXAS

Bend Saddlery
P.O. Box 38
Alpine, TX 79831
(800) 634-4502

Serves the ranch industry with custom-made saddles, chaps, belts, and Western gear.

Catalena Hats
203 North Main
Bryan, TX 77803
(409) 822-4423
Custom hats and renovations.

Daziers of Dallas
10750 Forest Lane
Dallas, TX 75243
(214) 340-5350
A total Southwest store.

Dennis Moreland Enterprises
P.O. Box 330
Goldthwaite, TX 76844
(800) 523-0970
Cowboy gear and tack.

Eclectic
918 West 12th Street
Austin, TX 78703
(512) 477-1863
Cowhide furniture and folk art.

Eddie Kimmel Custom Boots and Bags
Route 1, Box 36
Comanche, TX 76442
(915) 356-3197
Custom boots, bags, and belts.

Folk Art Gallery of the San Antonio Museum of Art
200 West Jones Avenue
San Antonio, TX 78215
(512) 978-8100
Texan, Mexican, and Latin American folk arts.

Hatatorium Hat Shop
25 North Chadbourne
San Angelo, TX 76903
(915) 655-9191
Western clothing, custom hats, and hat renovation.

Homestead
223 East Main
Fredericksburg, TX 78624
(512) 997-5551
Western Americana, custom linens, and great cowboy material at an adjunct shop—Rancho No Tengo.

Horse of a Different Color
140 West Sunset Road
San Antonio, TX 78209
(write for information)
Texas furniture and antiques, Mexican colonial art.

Jabberwocky
203 East Main
Fredericksburg, TX 78624
(512) 997-7071
Vintage quilts, linens, and other things of the West.

King Ranch Saddle Shop
201 East Kleberg
P.O. Box 1594
Kingsville, TX 78364-1594
(800) 282-KING
Associated with the giant ranch, they also make saddles and other cowboy gear.

Mike's Boot Shop
604 West Avenue
Wellington, TX 79095
(806) 447-5809
Handmade boots and repairs.

R. E. Donaho Saddle Shop
8 East Concho Avenue
San Angelo, TX 76903
(915) 655-3270
Maker of fine saddles and leather works.

Rimfire Forge
Box 1324
Marfa, TX 79843
(915) 729-4450
Custom-made bits and spurs.

Rocketbuster Boots
2905 Pershing
El Paso, TX 79903
(915) 562-1114
Colorful boots based on 1950s designs.

Sol del Rio
1020 Townshend
San Antonio, TX 78209
(512) 828-5555
Mexican folk arts.

Millard Spriggs
608½ East Holland
Alpine, TX 79830
(915) 837-7392
Millard Spriggs has been making boots for 41 years.

Stanley Boot Shop
1112 North Chadbourne
San Angelo, TX 76903
(915) 655-8226
Custom-made boots and styles and any way you like 'em.

Teddi Marks Antiques and Texas Longhorn Furniture
Box 208, Highway 6
Meridian, TX 76665
(817) 435-2173
American country, Indian, Western, and Southwestern antiques.

Tienda Guadalupe
1001 South Alamo
San Antonio, TX 78210
(512) 226-5873
Mexican and local Hispanic arts.

True West
Tyler and Teresa Beard
P.O. Box 148
Comanche, TX 76442
(915) 356-2140
Specializing in fine, historic cowboy material and Western Americana.

The Turquoise Door
903 West 12th Street
Austin, TX 78703
(512) 480-0618
Folk art and furnishings.

Wilson and Mengo Boots
(18 miles SW of Angelo on Highway 2335)
Box 424
Knickerbocker, TX 76939
(915) 944-4961
Handmade cowboy gear including silk scarves, spurs, bits, and bed tarps.

WYOMING

Alpine Woodworks
P.O. Box 261
Alpine, WY 83128
(307) 654-7658
Lodgepole fine furniture.

Cabin Fever
3525 North Moose
Wilson Road
Jackson, WY 83001
(307) 733-0274
Experienced in Western interior design; retail shop with furnishings and accessories.

Cattle Kate
Box 572
Wilson, WY 83014
(307) 733-7414
Clothing designed to give the look of the Old West.

Elkhorn Design
70 Cache Street
Jackson, WY 83001
(307) 733-4655
Horn furniture.

King's Saddlery
184 North Main
Sheridan, WY 82801
(800) 443-8919
(307) 672-2702
Ropes, bits, boots, and gear.

Timberline Log Furniture
P.O. Box 292-WH
Big Piney, WY 83113
(307) 276-3570
Log furniture and other Western styles.

Unc's Boot Shop
28 East Broadway
Jackson, WY 83001
(307) 733-4511
Custom boots.

THE OLD WEST

ALASKA

Klondike Gold Rush National Historic Park
P.O. Box 517
Second and Broadway
Skagway, AK 99840
(907) 983-2921
Housed in a late 19th-century White Pass and Yukon Route Railroad depot, the museum features gold rush items and a research library.

Trail of the '98 Museum
7th and Spring Streets
Skagway, AK 99840
(907) 983-2420
Museum interprets the gold rush era of Alaskan history through photos, documents, artifacts, and equipment used by stampeders along the White Pass and Chikoot trails.

ARIZONA

The Amerind Foundation, Inc.
P.O. Box 248
Dragoon Road
Dragoon, AZ 85609
(602) 586-3666
Archeological and ethnological collections of the Southwest and Great Plains and other interpretive materials including paintings, sculpture, and decorative arts.

Arizona Historical Society
949 East Second Street
Tucson, AZ 85719
(602) 628-5774
Historical museum with major collections of Arizona-related artifacts and research materials.

Arizona State Museum
University of Arizona
Park Avenue at University
Tucson, AZ 85721
(602) 621-6281
Collections focus on Southwestern archeology, ethnohistory, ethnology, and natural history.

Bisbee Mining and Historical Museum
#5 Copper Queen Plaza
P.O. Box 14
Bisbee, AZ 85603
(602) 432-7071
A museum devoted to the impact and history of mining, located in this old mining area.

Chiricahua National Monument
Dos Cabezas Route
Box 6500
Willcox, AZ 85643
(602) 824-3560
Natural history museum in a historic area that includes Faraway Ranch and Stafford cabin.

Desert Caballeros Western Museum
21 North Frontier Street
P.O. Box 1446
Wickenburg, AZ 85358
(602) 684-2272
Period rooms, pioneer collections, and mining history.

Hubbell Trading Post National Historic Site
Box 150
Ganado, AZ 86505
(602) 755-3254
Navajo reservation trading post named for its founder and dean of the traders, John Lorenzo Hubbell. Historic home, post, and active sales in Navajo art and crafts.

Museum of Northern Arizona
Fort Valley Road
Route 4, Box 720
Flagstaff, AZ 86001
(602) 774-5211
Prehistory and ethnography of the Southwest, zoological specimens, and Southwestern Anglo and Indian art. Monthly activities include expeditions into the backcountry of the Colorado Plateau.

Stradling Museum of the Horse
350 McKeown Avenue
P.O. Box 413
Patagonia, AZ 85624
(602) 394-2264
Through the years Ms. Stradling collected horse equipment, saddles, harnesses,

bits, spurs as well as paintings, books, and vehicles.

Tombstone Courthouse State Historic Park
219 Toughnut Street
P.O. Box 216
Tombstone, AZ 85638
(602) 457-3311
Tombstone history and memorabilia from this famous little town.

CALIFORNIA

California Historical Society
2090 Jackson Street
San Francisco, CA 94109
(415) 567-1848
The society sponsors house tours and travel programs related to state history.

Craft and Folk Art Museum
5814 Wilshire Boulevard
Los Angeles, CA 90036
(213) 937-5544
Active programs, exhibit facility, education divisions, and membership.

El Pueblo de los Angeles Historic Park
845 North Alameda Street
Los Angeles, CA 90012
(213) 628-1274
Once a little Spanish town, this museum focuses on the early history of one of America's largest urban areas, L.A. Historic buildings, manuscript collections, architectural drawings, photographs, and archeological collections.

Gene Autry Western Heritage Museum
4700 Zoo Drive
Los Angeles, CA 90027-1462
(213) 667-2000
Perhaps the best museum of cowboy history and Western life to be found. Active program division, museum shop, and newsletter.

Jack London State Historic Park
20 East Spain Street
Sonoma, CA 95476
(707) 938-5216
Located in a home of London's near Glen Ellen, the park includes ruins of his mansion Wolf House and collections.

Monterey State Historic Park
525 Polk Street
Monterey, CA 93940
(408) 649-7118
Historic park museum consisting of 12 buildings and sites, including the Cooper-Holera Adobe, the Casa Soberanes, and Casa Gutierrez.

National Hispanic Museum
421 N. Avenue 19, 4th Floor
P.O. Box 985377
Los Angeles, CA 90087
(213) 222-1349
Permanent displays and changing exhibits focus on the history of this major American ethnic group.

Roy Rogers and Dale Evans Museum
15650 Seneca Road
Victorville, CA 92392
(619) 243-4547
Explores the happy trails of this performing couple.

San Buenaventura Mission Museum
211 East Main Street
Ventura, CA 93001
(805) 643-4318
Part of the great chain of California missions, this museum focuses on the mission's history through historic collections of original and related artifacts.

San Fernando Mission
15151 San Fernando
Mission Boulevard
Mission Hills, CA 91345
(818) 361-0186
Historic buildings and collections re-create a part of early mission life.

COLORADO

"Buffalo Bill" Cody Memorial Museum and Grave
Lookout Mountain Road
Route 5, Box 950
Golden, CO 80401
(303) 526-0747
Exhibits on Cody's life, boyhood in Iowa and Kansas, the Pony Express, buffalo hunting, scouting, and Buffalo Bill's Wild West Show.

Colorado Springs Fine Arts Center
30 West Dale Street
Colorado Springs, CO 80903
(719) 634-5581
Major collection of Hispanic New Mexican material forms one part of this museum of art and culture in the Southwest.

Matchless Mine Museum
414 West 7th Street
Leadville, CO 80461
(719) 486-0371
Historical items relating to a famous mine.

Museum of Western Art
1727 Tremont Plaza
Denver, CO 80202
(303) 296-1880
Western American art including works by some of the greatest such as Bierstadt, Moran, Farny, Russell, Remington, Blumenschein, and O'Keeffe.

National Carvers Museum
14960 Woodcarver Road
Monument, CO 80132
(303) 481-2656
A museum founded to cultivate an understanding and appreciation of carving; includes over 4,000 carvings.

Pro Rodeo Hall of Champions and Museum of the American Cowboy
101 Pro Rodeo Drive
Colorado Springs, CO 80919
(303) 593-8840
Rodeo memorabilia from some of the all-time greats.

DISTRICT OF COLUMBIA

Smithsonian Institution
1000 Jefferson Drive
Washington, D.C. 20560
(202) 357-1300

A national museum with extensive collections and research facilities focusing on American history and culture, arts, and design.

IDAHO

Appaloosa Museum
5070 Highway 8 West
P.O. Box 8403
Moscow, ID 83843
(208) 882-5578
Devoted to the Appaloosa horse and the involvement of the Nez Percé Indians in the development of the breed.

Idaho Historical Society
610 North Julia Davis Drive
Boise, ID 83702
(208) 334-2120
Collections, library, and research on the state.

Nez Percé National Historic Park
Highway 95
P.O. Box 93
Spalding, ID 83551
(208) 843-2261
Located on an early mission site, park's collections include prehistory, pioneer, historic documents, and over 3,000 photos of the Native Americans of the region.

INDIANA

Eiteljorg Museum of American Indian and Western Art
500 West Washington Street
Indianapolis, IN 46204
(317) 636-9378
A new museum dedicated to Western America features collections of paintings, Indian art; with active program and education divisions, and an excellent museum shop.

KANSAS

Barbed Wire Museum
614 Main Street
La Crosse, KS 67548
(913) 222-3116
This museum, in a city billed as the Barbed Wire Capital of the World, claims to have the largest collection of barbed wire.

Boot Hill Museum
Front Street
Dodge City, KS 67801
(316) 227-8188
A museum located at the site of Boot Hill Cemetery has photographs, documents, and artifacts from Dodge City's early history.

Little Red Schoolhouse Living Library
303 East 12th Street
Beloit, KS 67420
(913) 738-2311
Early school books, manuscripts, school desks, and photographs document education in the West.

MONTANA

Cascade County Historical Society Museum and Archives
1400 First Avenue North
Great Falls, MT 59401
(406) 452-3462
An old corner store houses this museum and archives.

C. M. Russell Museum
400 13th Street North
Great Falls, MT 59401
(406) 727-8787
Art of the American West and especially that of Charlie Russell; also includes his studio and home.

Grant-Kohrs Ranch National Historic Site
¼ mile North
P.O. Box 790
Deer Lodge, MT 59722
(406) 846-2070
Historic site of a 23-room ranch house from the 1800s and bunkhouse, barns, and outbuildings. Collections of ranch equipment, programs, and tours.

Montana Historic Society
225 N. Roberts
Helena, MT 59620
(406) 444-2694
Wonderful photo archives with over 200,000 images, comprehensive newspaper collection, Montana history and exhibit space.

Museum of the Rockies
Montana State University
Bozeman, MT 59717
(406) 994-2251
Photo archives, art gallery, and exhibits relating to the natural history of the region.

National Bison Range
Moiese, MT 59824
(406) 644-2211
The range protects one of the most important of the remaining herds of the American bison.

Old Montana Prison
1106 Main Street
Deer Lodge, MT 59722
(406) 846-3111
Twelve structures surrounded by an 1893 sandstone wall served as a territorial and state prison from 1871 to 1979.

Yellowstone Days Exhibition Depot Center
200 West Park Street
P.O. Box 1319
Livingston, MT 59047
(406) 222-2300
Old West displays open mid-May to mid-October.

NEBRASKA

Historic Homes Tour
Cass County Historical Society Museum
646 Main Street
Plattsmouth, NE 68048
(402) 296-4770
Offers guided tours of restored historical homes and buildings.

Museum of the Fur Trade
U.S. Highway 20
Chadron, NE 69337
(308) 432-2843
Collections of trade goods and other materials relevant to the commerce and daily life of trappers and traders.

Willa Cather Historical Center
Nebraska State
Historical Society
338 North Webster
P.O. Box 326
Red Cloud, NE 68970
(402) 746-3285
Willa Cather letters, first editions, photographs, and artifacts. Includes a library, archive, and reading room.

NEW MEXICO

Bandelier National Monument
State Route 4
Los Alamos, NM 87544
(505) 672-3861
Archeological and ethnological items of Pueblo Indians of the

Pajarito Plateau, as well as plant and animal specimens of the Jemez Mountains. Fascinating ruins and great hiking trails.

Fort Union National Monument
Route 161
Watrous, NM 87753
(505) 425-8025
On the edge of the Plains and along the route of the Santa Fe Trail, the haunting remains of a large fort.

Gadsden Museum
Barker Road and Highway 28
Box 147
Mesilla, NM 88046
(505) 526-6293
This local museum explores the history of a family and its importance to the history of the region.

El Morro National Monument
Highway 53-43
Ramah, NM 87321
(505) 783-4226
Site has a glorious Inscription Rock with signatures from 1605–1906 as well as significant archeological ruins.

El Rancho de las Golondrinas
County Road 54
Route 14, Box 214
Santa Fe, NM 87505
(505) 471-2261
"The Ranch of the Swallows" was founded in the early 1700s as a stopping place along the Camino Real. Restored buildings recreate early Hispanic life on this living-history museum.

Kit Carson Foundation
222 Ledoux Street
Drawer CCC
Taos, NM 87571
(505) 758-0505
The foundation administers a number of historic properties in the Taos area including Kit Carson's home and the massive Martinez Hacienda.

Millicent Rogers Museum
Museum Road 4 miles north of Taos
P.O. Box A
Taos, NM 87571
(505) 758-2642
A charming small museum that explores Native American and Hispanic arts in a serious and professional fashion.

Museum of International Folk Art
706 Camino Lejo
P.O. Box 2087
Santa Fe, NM 87503
(505) 827-6350

Major holdings of Hispanic New Mexican textiles and religious folk art as well as enormous collections of folk art from around the world, including the Girard Collection.

San Juan County Archeological Research Center and Library of the Salmon Ruins
975 U.S. Highway 64
Farmington, NM 87401
(505) 632-2013
Collections range from the historical to the archeological, including a 1903 root cellar, corral, barn, and adobe home.

NORTH DAKOTA

Theodore Roosevelt Medora Foundation
Box 198
Medora, ND 58645
(701) 623-4444
A re-created 1880s boom town with museums, historic buildings, and accommodations. Annual Dakota Cowboy poetry gathering is held here on Memorial Day weekend.

OKLAHOMA

Chisholm Trail Museum
605 Zellers Avenue
Kingfisher, OK 73750
(405) 375-5176
The museum recaptures the era of the cattle drive using old maps, vintage photographs, and cowboy ranch equipment.

Museum of the Great Plains
601 Ferris Avenue
P.O. Box 68
Lawton, OK 73502
(405) 353-5675
A regional history museum

with exhibits exploring the Plains Indian and white settlement history.

Museum of the Western Prairie
1100 North Hightower
P.O. Box 574
Altus, OK 73521
(405) 482-1044
Early agricultural and ranching tools, Native American collections, and archival holdings.

National Cowboy Hall of Fame and Western Heritage Center
1700 NE 63rd Street
Oklahoma City, OK 73111
(405) 478-2250
This major museum celebrating the West includes a frontier town, the Hall of Fame of Great Westerners, and the Rodeo Hall of Fame as well as a collection of art by foremost Western artists.

Tom Mix Museum
721 N. Delaware
Dewey, OK 74029
(918) 534-1555
After serving with the Rough Riders in the Spanish-American War, breaking wild horses, and serving as the marshall of Dewey, Tom Mix broke into silent films. On display are personal effects and stills from the films.

OREGON

Burrows House and Log Cabin Museum
545 S.W. Ninth Street
Newport, OR 97365
(503) 265-7509
Explores Indian and pioneer life of the region.

Oregon Historical Society
1230 S.W. Park Avenue
Portland, OR 97205
(503) 222-1741
This historical center is a major repository for maps and early photographs of the state and a library of Oregon history.

SOUTH DAKOTA

Prairie Homestead
HCR 01, Box 51
Philip, SD 57567
(605) 386-4523
A 1909 sod home with some of the original furnishings shows life of the sodbusters.

TEXAS

Bullfight Museum
5001 Alameda
El Paso, TX 79905
(915) 772-2711
Material and exhibits relating to the history and development of the sport.

Cultural Heritage Centers
Mexican, Asian, Native, and European American
Thomas A. Edison School Office 219
Dallas, TX 75212
(214) 630-1680
Arts and crafts, programs, and festivals pertaining to these various ethnic groups so important to the West.

Deaf Smith County Museum
400 Sampson
Box 1007
Hereford, TX 79045
(806) 364-4338
Historic buildings and early ranching years.

Gish's Old West Museum
502 N. Milam
Fredericksburg, TX 78624
(512) 997-2794
A privately owned museum displays relics of the Old West in an Old West setting. There is no admission charge and no regular hours so give a call.

Institute of Texas Culture
801 South Bowie at Durango Boulevard
P.O. Box 1226
San Antonio, TX 78294
(512) 226-7651
An important institution for the interpretation of Texas history through its many ethnic groups. A public library and extensive photographic holdings as well as active public programing and exhibition schedules.

King Ranch Museum
P.O. Box 1090
Kingsville, TX 78364-1090
(512) 592-8055
Features a photographic essay of life on the King Ranch, plus a collection of antique coaches, vintage cars, saddles, and other historic exhibits.

Lyndon B. Johnson National Historic Park
Off Highway 290
P.O. Box 329
Johnson City, TX 78636
(512) 868-7128
Site includes reconstructed birthplace, boyhood home, as well as the LBJ Ranch.

Lone Star Brewery
600 Lone Star Boulevard
San Antonio, TX 78204
(512) 270-9467
Site of the Buckhorn Hall of Horns, Hall of Texas History, the Buckhorn Saloon, and the Halls of Feathers and Fins.

Llano Estacado Museum
Wayland University
Plainview, TX 79072
(806) 296-5521
Geological and archeological development of the Llano Estacado region.

National Cowgirl Hall of Fame and Western Heritage Center
515 Avenue B
P.O. Box 1742
Hereford, TX 79045
(806) 364-5252
Costumes, Western attire, and cowgirl photos and art.

National Wildflower Research Center
2600 FM 973 North
Austin, TX 78725
(512) 929-3600
Wildflower information is shared and collected for growers, gardeners, scientists, and lovers of flowers. Tours of the center are offered.

Ranching Heritage Center
4th and Indiana
Box 4040
Lubbock, TX 79409
(806) 742-2498
A 14-acre center with more than 30 historic structures from ranches throughout the state; illustrates the day-to-day existence of Texas ranchers from the 1830s to the 1920s.

San Antonio Missions
National Park Service
2202 Roosevelt Avenue
San Antonio, TX 78210-4919
(512) 229-5701
An impressive chain of Spanish missions along the San Antonio River; museums and active churches make up this major series of monuments.

Texas Memorial Museum
2400 Trinity
Austin, TX 78705
(512) 471-1604
Texas history, prehistory, and natural sciences.

Texas Ranger Hall of Fame and Museum
Fort Fisher Park, I35 and the Brazos River
P.O. Box 2570
Waco, TX 76702
(817) 754-1433

Texas Ranger historical papers, artifacts, and costumes as well as paintings and sculpture relating to the subject.

Texas and Southwestern Cattle Raisers Foundation
1301 West 7th
Fort Worth, TX 76102
(817) 332-6167
A small museum tells the history of the foundation and of brands for this association of the cattlemen.

Winedale Historical Center
University of Texas at Austin
FM Road 2714
P.O. Box 11
Round Top, TX 78954
(409) 278-3530
Historic houses with complete furnishings and decorative arts, folk art, tools, and agricultural implements pertaining to the German settlements of Texas. Active interpretive programs.

UTAH

Golden Spike National Historic Site
P.O. Box W
Brigham City, UT 84302
(801) 471-2209
First transcontinental railroad was completed here on May 10, 1869; collection documents railroad, construction, and workers.

Utah State Historical Society
300 Rio Grande
Salt Lake City, UT 84101
(801) 533-5755
Extensive library and geneological material housed in an old railroad station.

WASHINGTON

Washington State Historical Society
315 N. Stadium Way
Tacoma, WA 98403
Research library and exhibitions devoted to the state's history.

WYOMING

Bradford Brinton Memorial
239 Brinton Road
Box 23
Big Horn, WY 82833
(307) 672-3173
An historic ranch with a museum of art including works by Russell, Remington, and Audubon.

Buffalo Bill Historical Center
720 Sheridan Avenue
P.O. Box 1000
Cody, WY 82414
(307) 587-4771

The museum complex is composed of the Buffalo Bill Museum, Winchester Arms Museum, Whitney Gallery of Western Art, Plains Indian Museum, garden areas, and special exhibitions.

Fort Caspar Museum
4001 Fort Casper Road
Casper, WY 82604
(307) 235-8462
During the summer months this museum has an active schedule of events including a mountain man rendezvous and Western history speakers.

Grand Teton National Park
P.O. Drawer 170
Moose, WY 83012
(307) 543-2484
At this spectacular park can be found an art museum and various guided walks, films, and other cultural events.

Jackson Hole Museum
105 N. Glenwood
Jackson Hole, WY 83001
(307) 733-9605
Historic walking tours of downtown Jackson and a museum of the Old West.

Pryor Mountain Wild Horse Range
Lovell Area Chamber of Commerce
287 E. Main, Box 295
Lovell, WY 82431
(307) 548-7552
A wild horse refuge.

South Pass City
Wyoming Recreation Commission
Cheyenne, WY 82002
(307) 332-3684
A once-thriving gold camp including 24 original buildings with period furnishings. Tours are offered.

Wyoming Territorial Prison
P.O. Box 1631
Laramie, WY 82070
(307) 745-6161
The prison where Butch

Cassidy served is part of this park, which also includes a mining camp, pioneer ranch, and Old West town.

HIDEOUTS AND WATERING HOLES

ARIZONA

Canyon de Chelly National Monument
P.O. Box 588
Chinle, AZ 86503
(602) 674-5436
A spot of deep historic and religious significance to Native Americans; providing guided tours, camping, lodging, and horseback riding in a sublime location.

Circle Z Ranch
Patagonia, AZ 85624
(602) 287-2091
A guest ranch consisting of historic Spanish adobe guest cottages, a lodge, and cantina on ranchlands bordered by the Coronado National Forest.

Grand Canyon National Park
Box 129
Grand Canyon, AZ 86023
(602) 638-7769
One of the "grandest" sights on earth provides unparalleled beauty and opportunities for intense physical exercise and fascinating encounters with the remains of ancient cultures.

Grapevine Canyon Ranch, Inc.
P.O. Box 302
Pearce, AZ 85625
(602) 826-3185
An intimate guest ranch with emphasis on horseback riding and outdoor activities.

Lazy K Bar Guest Ranch
8401 Scenic Drive
Tucson, AZ 85743
(602) 744-3050
Guest ranch with numerous activities including swimming, riding, dancing, volleyball, and tennis.

Old West Outfitters
14255 N. 79th Street
Scottsdale, AZ 85260
(602) 951-9022
Real cattle drives in various states that men, women, and children can join for an authentic Western experience.

CALIFORNIA

Ranch Vacations
P.O. Box 7041
Lake Tahoe, CA 95730
(800) 222-4229, operator 74
Complete guide to more than 200 dude, cattle, resort, fly fishing, and cross-country skiing ranches in the United States and Canada.

Spanish Springs Ranch
c/o Spanish Springs Information Center
1102 Second Street
San Rafael, CA 94901
(800) 228-0279
(800) 272-8282 (in CA)
A working cattle ranch offering camping, cattle or horse drives, as well as winter sports and sleigh rides.

COLORADO

American Wilderness Experience
Box 1486
Boulder, CO 80306
(800) 444-0099
Offers many types of vacations including riding, cross-country skiing, or a Yellowstone Park snowmobile tour.

Cherokee Park Ranch
P.O. Box 97
Livermore, CO 80536
(800) 628-0949
(303) 493-6522
The ranch sits in valley of the Cache La Poudre River. Welcoming guests for over a century, the ranch provides renovated cabins with modern conveniences without losing the feel of the Old West.

Colorado Trails Ranch
Box 848
Durango, CO 81302
(800) 323-3833
(303) 247-5055
Many activities are offered at this ranch including horseback riding, tennis, archery, fishing, hayrides, rafting, and music and dance.

Dude Ranchers Associations
P.O. Box 471
La Porte, CO 80535
(303) 493-7623
Publishes a yearly directory of its members along with a description of each ranch.

North Fork Ranch
Box B
Shawnee, CO 80475
(303) 838-9873
A ranch on the banks of the South Platte River. Activities include hiking, riding, rafting, pack trips, square dancing, and skit nights.

Powderhorn Guest Ranch
Powderhorn, CO 81243
(303) 641-0220
A small family-owned ranch with riding and fishing.

IDAHO

Idaho Afloat
Box 542
Grangeville, ID 83530
(208) 983-2414
Rowing and riding are major activities on a six-day combination adventure.

Twin Peaks Ranch
P.O. Box 951
Salmon, ID 83467
(208) 894-2290
The ranch sits amidst the Rockies and offers riding, float trips, and fishing.

Wapiti Meadow Ranch
H.C. 72
Cascade, ID 83611
(208) 382-4336
A wilderness retreat in the heart of the Idaho's Salmon River Mountains.

KANSAS

Flint Hills Overland Wagon Train Trips
Box 1076
El Dorado, KS 67042
(316) 321-6300
An overnight trail ride in covered wagons recreates the trips of early pioneers.

MONTANA

Beartooth Plateau Outfitters
Box 1127
Main Street
Cooke City, MT 59020
(406) 838-2328
(406) 445-2293
An area headquarters for fishing tackle that also offers half-day rides, pack trips, and gold-panning tours.

Double Diamond Guest Ranch
Box 501 Highway 83
Condon, MT 59826
(800) 367-3612
A stay at the ranch includes all meals, your own horse, and other activities including canoeing, hiking, swimming, and fishing.

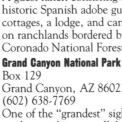

Firehole Ranch
West Yellowstone, MT
For reservations, Rivermeadows
P.O. Box 347
Wilson, WY 83014
(307) 733-3674
Great fly fishing in the tradition of the Crescent H in Jackson, Wyoming.

Glacier National Park
West Glacier, MT 59936
(406) 888-5441
In the Northern Rockies, Glacier is among America's most beautiful parks, filled with lakes and mountains and with one of the most extraordinary roads through the mountains.

Glacier Wilderness Guides
Box 535
West Glacier, MT 59936
(800) 521-RAFT
Guides lead raft trips down the Middle and North Forks of the Flathead River and offer other trips on horseback or on foot.

Izaak Walton Inn
P.O. Box 653
Essex, MT 59916
(406) 888-5700
A year-round hotel located at the edge of Glacier National Park. Not only close to wilderness but also a great spot for railroad buffs since it was once a hotel for those who built and worked on the Great Northern.

Mountain Sky Guest Ranch
Box 1128
Bozeman, MT 59715
(800) 548-3392
A luxurious ranch offering pool and spa, workout room, stocked casting pond, and riding.

Off the Beaten Track
109 East Main Street
Suite 4
Bozeman, MT 59715
(406) 586-1311
This unusual travel service can customize a trip to include a guest ranch, fishing, or a wilderness pack trip.

Denny Salveson
Box 182
Red Lodge, MT 59068
(406) 446-2353
Outfitter that offers expeditions to Old Faithful, the Continental Divide, Twister Falls, and other spots in the backcountry.

63 Ranch
Box WH979
Livingston, MT 59047
(406) 222-0570

A working dude ranch listed on the National Register of Historic Places, offers 100 miles of riding trails, trout fishing, and excursions to nearby Livingston.

Travel Montana
Deer Lodge, MT 59722
(800) 541-1447
A branch of the State Department of Commerce, this organization provides free maps, guides to motels, resorts, outfitters, and travel services.

Wild Horse Island
Montana Department of Fish, Wildlife and Parks
P.O. Box 67
Kalispell, MT 59903
(406) 752-5501
Accessible only by boat, the island is home to bighorn sheep, deer, and mink.

NEW MEXICO

Dorsey Mansion Ranch
HCR 62, Box 42, Chico Route
Raton, NM 87740
(505) 375-2222
Once home to a cattle baron, the ranch now is a bed and breakfast offering tours of this unusual, elaborate log cabin.

Organ Mountains Recreation Area
A.B. Cox Visitor Center
1800 Marques Street
Las Cruces, NM 88803
(505) 522-1219
Marked trails and picnic areas in dramatic mountains.

Rojo Tours
228 Old Santa Fe Trail
Santa Fe, NM 87501
(505) 983-8333
An organization that plans trips in New Mexico.

NEVADA

Great Basin National Park
Highway 488
Baker, NV 89311
(702) 234-7331
The newest national park offers great opportunities for the

outdoors person. Guided tours, evening programs on archeology, geology, and botany of the region.

NORTH DAKOTA

Logging Camp Ranch
HC 1, Box 27
Bowman, ND 58623
(701) 279-5501
Wildlife in the region of this active ranch includes deer, burrowing owls, and wild turkey.

Peaceful Valley Ranch
Box 197
Medora, ND 58645
(701) 623-4496
Day-long and overnight horseback excursions.

OREGON

Crater Lake National Park
P.O. Box 7
Crater Lake, OR 97604
(503) 594-2211
A spectacular lake formed by volcanic action, in the Oregon wilderness.

SOUTH DAKOTA

Badlands National Park
P.O. Box 6
Interior, SD 57750
(605) 433-5361
At this park in addition to wonderful scenery the staff offers educational programs such as night prowls, night sky observation, and fossil preparation demonstrations.

TEXAS

Amarillo Ranch Roundup
Convention and
Visitor Council
P.O. Box 9480
Amarillo, TX 79105
(800) 692-1338
A genuine cowboy experience including real cowboy grub, a

ranch rodeo, and sleeping under the stars.

Big Bend National Park
Big Bend, TX 79834
(915) 477-2251
At the southern tip of Texas, a spectacular park where the Rio Grande cuts a deep canyon.

Chihuahuan Desert Research Institute and Visitor Center
P.O. Box 1334
Alpine, TX 79831
(915) 837-8370
Botanical garden, nature trails, and a conservation center devoted to this desert region.

Lazy Hills Guest Ranch
Box G
Ingram, TX 78025
(512) 367-5600
A homey, family-oriented ranch in the Texas Hill Country, with emphasis on hiking and riding.

UTAH

Hondoo Rivers and Trails
Box 98
Torrey, UT 84775
(801) 425-3519
Pack trips to explore the archeology, geology, and history of Utah.

Monument Valley Navajo Tribal Park
Box 93
Monument Valley, UT 84536
(801) 727-3287
The grand mesa landscape made famous in films of John Huston.

WYOMING

Akers Ranch
81 Inez Ranch
Douglas, WY 82633
(307) 358-3741
An east-central Wyoming working cattle ranch offers visitors a chance to mend a fence, feed a calf, or help bake some bread.

Barker-Ewing River Trips
45 West Broadway
Box 3032-B
Jackson, WY 83001
(307) 733-1000
Float trips and whitewater adventures.

Bar-J Ranch
P.O. Box 220
Wilson, WY 83014
(307) 733-3370
A chuck wagon provides the spirit of the Old West; along with the Western meal is entertainment led by the Bar-J

Wrangler, including cowboy songs, yodeling, cowboy poetry, and ranch-style humor.

Bar-T-Five Corral
Cache Creek Road
Jackson, WY 83001
(307) 733-3534
(307) 733-5386
Scenic guided trail rides in Cache Creek Canyon located in Bridger Teton National Forest. Covered wagon cookouts are also offered.

Crescent H Ranch
c/o River Meadows
P.O. Box 730
Wilson, WY 83014
(307) 733-3674
(307) 733-2841
Great fishing with expert guides to teach and lead, a classic main lodge full of lodgepole and horn furniture, and charming cabins make this a serene and lovely spot for those seeking a chance to fish.

Devils Tower National Monument
Box 8
Devils Tower, WY 82714
(307) 467-5370
This surreal rock formation sprouting up out of the landscape has a museum exploring the culture, geology, and botany of the region.

Equitour
Bitteroot Ranch
Rte. 66, Box 1402
Dubois, WY 82513
(307) 455-3363
(800) 545-0019
Week-long rides on Wyoming's outlaw trail retrace the steps of Butch Cassidy and others.

Grand Teton Lodge Company
Grand Teton National Park
P.O. Box 240
Moran, WY 83013
(307) 543-2855
(307) 733-2811
This concessionaire operates Jackson Lake Lodge, Jenny Lake Lodge, and Colter Bay Village. In addition it offers fishing trips, float trips, and guided trail rides.

Grand Teton National Park
P.O. Drawer 170
Moose, WY 83012
One of America's most spectacular mountain ranges provides the setting for this national park offering boating, fishing, hiking, riding, and mountaineering.

Great Plains Wildlife Research Institute
P.O. Box 7580
Jackson, WY 83001
(307) 733-2623
(307) 733-1615
Regional wildlife safaris giving direct exposure to the habits and ecology of animals.

Grey Horse Outfitters
Adventures West
Mountain Camp
P.O. Box 428
Mills, WY 82644
(307) 266-4868
(307) 472-2122
Historic wagon train trips, float trips, overland trail stagecoach trip, and other outdoor trips.

Heart Six Ranch
P.O. Box 70
Moran, WY 83013
(307) 543-2477
(307) 733-6994
Float trips along the Snake River, wildlife floats, and fishing trips.

Hidden Valley Ranch
153 Hidden Valley Road,
Southfork
Cody, WY 82414
(307) 587-5090
Offering a wrangler school where skills relevant to riding are taught.

High Island Guest Ranch
Box 71
Hamilton Dome, WY 82427
(307) 352-2591
A working ranch with guest facilities. During the summer the ranch has several 40-mile cattle drives.

Lazy L and B Ranch
Dubois, WY 82513
(307) 455-2839
Dude ranch with activities such as riding and fishing.

Mill Iron Ranch
P.O. Box 951
Jackson, WY 83001
(307) 733-6390
Private fishing ranch that provides fly fishing school and float trips.

Moose Head Ranch
Moose, WY 83012
(307) 733-3141
A privately owned ranch within the boundary of the Grand Teton National Park, with riding, hiking, cookouts, and fishing.

National Park Tours
Gray Line of Jackson Hole
P.O. Box 411
Jackson, WY 83001
(800) 443-6133
Summer sightseeing program with overnight stays and packages to both Yellowstone and Grand Teton.

S Bar S Enterprises
P.O. Box 717
Cowley, WY 82420
(307) 548-6418
Tours through the Bighorn Canyon National Recreation area.

Signal Mountain Lodge
P.O. Box 50
Moran, WY 83013
(307) 543-2831
A semirustic lakeside resort inside Grand Teton National Park.

Spahn's Bighorn Mountain Bed and Breakfast
P.O. Box 579
Big Horn, WY 82833
(307) 674-8150
A main lodge and secluded cabins, wildlife, hunting and fishing, walking trails, and cross-country skiing.

T Cross Ranch
P.O. Box 638
Dubois, WY 82513
(307) 455-2206
The ranch was homesteaded in 1917 and has operated as a dude ranch since 1930. Surrounding lands are national forest.

Teton Trail Rides
Box 1350
Jackson, WY 83001
(307) 733-6409
Ride with a guide in the Grand Tetons, one hour to all day.

Thermopolis Hot Springs
220 Park Street
Thermopolis, WY 82443
(307) 864-2636
Adjacent to Hot Springs State Park, here are mineral baths and thermal swimming pools open to the public all year.

Triangle X Ranch
Moose, WY 83012
(307) 733-2183
An authentic dude ranch complete with riding, float trips, hiking, and fishing.

Westbank Anglers
P.O. Box 523
Teton Village, WY 83025
(800) 922-3474
(307)733-6483
Guided fly fishing trips.

Yellowstone Adventure
Horse Creek Ranch
P.O. Box 3878
Jackson Hole, WY 83001
(307) 733-6556
Off the beaten path for overnight pack trips, horseback tours, and backcountry pack and fishing trips.

Yellowstone National Park
Yellowstone National Park,
WY 82190-9989
(307) 344-7311
America's first national park occupies the northwest corner of Wyoming.

RENDEZVOUS, RODEOS, AND GATHERINGS

ARIZONA

Cowboy Classics
Arizona National
Livestock Show
1826 McDowell Road
Phoenix, AZ 85007
(602) 258-8568
Western art and gear show and sale, held in January. Cowboy poets, musicians, and storytellers; in conjunction with the livestock show.

Old-Fashioned Harvest Festival
Phoenix Chamber
of Commerce
805 North Second Street
Phoenix, AZ 85004
(602) 254-5521
Thanksgiving Day celebration held in a restored pioneer community.

Parada del Sol and Rodeo
Scottsdale Chamber
of Commerce
P.O. Box 129
Scottsdale, AZ 85252
(602) 945-8481
Horsemanship exhibitions, parties, and parades; late January and early February.

Smoki Celebration
P.O. Box 123
Prescott, AZ 86302
(602) 445-2000
(602) 445-1230
An early-August city celebration in this most Western of towns.

Tucson Rodeo—La Fiesta de los Vaqueros
Tucson Rodeo
Committee, Inc.
P.O. Box 11006
Tucson, AZ 85734
(602) 294-8896
Held annually in February, this is the largest mid-winter outdoor rodeo on the professional circuit and includes the world's longest nonmotorized parade.

CALIFORNIA

Calaveras County Fair and Jumping Frog Jubilee
Chamber of Commerce
Angels Camp, CA 95222
(209) 736-4444
Features the renowned frog-jumping contest inspired by Mark Twain's tale; mid-May.

Calico Days
California Chamber
of Commerce
455 Capitol Mall
Sacramento, CA 95814
(916) 443-3771
A celebration of an 1880s boom town with gunfight skits, burro runs, and square dancing; mid-October.

California Rodeo
1034 North Main Street
Salinas, CA 93902
(408) 757-2951
One of the classic rodeos with events including cutting horse races and wild horse races; late July.

Christmas in Monterey
Monterey Peninsula
Chamber of Commerce
P.O. Box 1770
380 Alvarado
Monterey, CA 93942
(408) 649-1770
The community re-creates the early years with tours, Spanish carols, and period decorations.

Grand National Rodeo
Horse Show and
Livestock Exhibition
Cow Palace
P.O. Box 34206
San Francisco, CA 94134
(415) 469-6000

A major rodeo and exhibition running for 10 days; late October.

International Mariachi Festival
Director of Marketing Services
MCA Universal Studios
100 Universal City Plaza
Universal City, CA 91608
(818) 777-3953
A Hispanic music festival; mid-September.

Mule Days Celebration in Bishop
Southern California
Visitors Council
705 West Seventh Street
Los Angeles, CA 90017
(619) 873-8405
Late May sees Bishop emerge as the Mule Capital of the World. Mule shows and sales and naming of the World Champion Mule.

Pioneer Days in Fallbrook
San Diego Convention
and Visitors Bureau
1200 Third Avenue, Suite 824
San Diego, CA 92101
(619) 232-3101
Rodeo, parade, pancake breakfast, booths, and country-western dances; September.

San Luis Rey Fiesta and Barbecue
San Diego Convention
and Visitors Bureau
1200 Third Avenue, Suite 824
San Diego, CA 92101
(619) 232-3101
Blessing of the animals, crafts, music, dancing, and a barbecue; late July.

Santa Ysabel Mission Fiesta and Pit Barbecue
Southern California
Visitors Council
705 West Seventh Street
Los Angeles, CA 90017
(213) 629-0602
Caballeros, mariachis, barbecue, and Indian dances; mid-June.

Whiskey Flats Days
Kernville Chamber
of Commerce
Box 397
Kernville, CA 93238
(619) 376-2629
Celebrating gold rush days when the town was known as Whiskey Flats. Fiddlers, frog jumping, greased pig contest, Boot Hill epitaph writing contest, and mule races; mid-February.

Woodcarver's Jamboree
San Diego Convention
and Visitors Bureau
Department WD
1200 Third Avenue
San Diego, CA 92101
(619) 232-3101
Juried show of woodcarvings;
July.

World Championship Chili Cookoff
International Chili Society
P.O. Box 2966
Newport Beach, CA 92663
(714) 631-1780
The culmination of a series of
regional championships; late
October.

World's Largest Salmon Barbecue
Salmon Restoration
Association of California
P.O. Box 1448
Fort Bragg, CA 95437
(707) 964-2313
Features more than 5,000
pounds of salmon caught in
local waters and served to
visitors; late July.

COLORADO

National Western Stock Show Festival
1325 East 46th Avenue
Denver, CO 80216
(303) 297-1166
For nine days in January a
major show of prize livestock,
rodeo, entertainment, and
crafts.

Pack Burro Race and Festival
Chamber of Commerce
Box 312
Fairplay, CO 80440
(719) 539-2068
The main event is a race to see
who can ride, push, or pull
their burro, carrying all the
equipment miners used to use,
over a 13,000-foot pass; late
July to early August.

Professional Rodeo Cowboys Association
101 Pro Rodeo Drive
Colorado Springs, CO 80919
(719) 593-8840
This association can provide
information about rodeo events
held throughout the country.

Western Folklore Festival
Adams County Chamber
of Commerce
5911 North Washington Street
Denver, CO 80216
(303) 534-8500
Held in conjunction with the
Western Folklore Conference,
the festival offers a mixture of
scholarly discussion and

performance of traditional
music and dancing.

IDAHO

National Oldtime Fiddlers' Contest
8 East Idaho Street
Weiser, ID 83672
(208) 549-0450
The granddaddy of such
contests features more than 300
contestants ranging in age from
5 to 95; six days in June.

Northern Rockies Folk Festival
P.O. Box 656
Sun Valley, ID 83353
(208) 622-9371
As the name implies, a folk
festival for the region; late July
to early August.

INDIANA

Pioneer Craft Days
Conner Prairie
Pioneer Settlement
30 Conner Lane
Noblesville, IN 46060
(317) 776-6004
Pioneer crafts demonstrated
from candle dipping to shingle
making; early June.

MONTANA

Miles City Bucking Horse
901 Main Street
Miles City, MT 59301
(406) 232-2890
One of the most Western of all
rodeos with parades, cowboy
poetry gathering, and can-can
dancers; May.

Western Days
Chamber of Commerce
Box 2519
Billings, MT 59103
(406) 252-4016
Traditional Wild West
activities highlight this
community festival; mid-July.

Wild Horse Stampede
Wolf Point Chamber
of Commerce
Box 237
Wolf Point, MT 59201
(406) 653-2012
The oldest annual rodeo in the
state, with top performers
competing; July.

NEVADA

Cowboy Poetry Gathering
Western Folklife Center
P.O. Box 888
Elko, NV 89801
(702) 738-7508
A working cowboy's cultural
event celebrating the old
tradition of writing and reciting

poetry about life on the range.
Also features cowboy folk arts
and music; late January to early
February.

National Finals Rodeo in Las Vegas, Nevada
Pro Rodeo Cowboys
Association
101 Pro Rodeo Drive
Colorado Springs, CO 80919
(702) 457-4664 (Las Vegas
Chamber of Commerce)
This is the big one for the
professional rodeo riders, held
indoors for nine days; early
December.

National Hollering Contest
P.O. Box 528
Jackpot, NV 89825
(702) 755-2259
Held in a canyon south of
Jackpot. The judges determine
the winner based on range,
endurance, and tone qualities;
early July.

Reno Rodeo
Reno Livestock Event Center
P.O. Box 12335
Reno, NV 89510
(800) 876-4849
(702) 329-3877
Daredeviling against a desert
backdrop; late June.

NEW MEXICO

Aspen Festival and Paul Bunyan Days in Eagle Nest
Tourist Division, New Mexico
Department of Development
113 Washington Avenue
Santa Fe, NM 87503
(505) 827-0291
A fall festival in late
September, with log rolling,
jousting, axe throwing,
chopping, pole climbing, and a
barbecue.

Cowboy Octoberfest
Chamber of Commerce
1301 White Sands Boulevard
Box 518
Alamogordo, NM 88310
(505) 437-6120
Ghost town tours, arts and
crafts show, pageants, chuck
wagon dinners, and fiddlers'
contest; October.

Fiesta
Chamber of Commerce
Drawer 1
Taos, NM 87571
(505) 758-3873
Fiesta in celebration of the
feast days of Santa Anna and
Santiago; late July.

Fiesta de Santa Fe
P.O. Box 4516
Santa Fe, NM 87504
(505) 988-7575
Commemorating the
Reconquest by Don Diego de
Vargas, this is among the oldest
of America's community
celebrations. This early
September religious and secular
event includes the burning of
Zozobra (Old Man Gloom),
music and dance, and a series
of processions and parades.

Mayfair
Chamber of Commerce
P.O. Box 125
Cloudcroft, NM 88317
Horseshoe tournaments, rodeo,
chuck wagon dinners, and hay
rides; late May.

Old Taos Trade Fair
Martinez Hacienda
P.O. Box Drawer CCC
Taos, NM 87571
(505) 758-0505
Mountain men and their crafts,
music, lectures, food, and craft
demonstrations bring back the
frontier life of Taos; late
September.

Palace Mountain Man Rendezvous and Buffalo Roast
Museum of New Mexico
Palace of the Governors
Box 2087
Santa Fe, NM 87504
(505) 827-6474
Mountain man trade fair,
muzzle-loading shoots, music,
parade, and buffalo roast in the
City Different; August.

Rails and Trails Days
Las Vegas Chamber
of Commerce
Box 148
Las Vegas, NM 87701
(505) 425-8631
Fiddle contest, train rides,
rodeo, and visits to the Santa
Fe Trail; early June.

Spanish Market
Spanish Colonial Arts Society
Box 1611
Santa Fe, NM 87504
(505) 983-4038
Traditional Southwest Spanish
crafts offered for sale on the
plaza for two days; late July.

The Whole Enchilada Fiesta
Las Cruces Chamber
of Commerce
P.O. Box CLC
Las Cruces, NM 88004
(505) 524-1968
Witness the construction of the
world's largest enchilada as well
as theatrical productions,
concerts, and arts and crafts;
early October.

OKLAHOMA

Cimarron Territory Celebration
Beaver Chamber of Commerce
P.O. Box 878
Beaver, OK 73932
(405) 625-4726
Beaver is the Cow Chip Capital
of the World and site of the
championship throwing
contest; late April.

International Professional Rodeo Association
P.O. Box 645
Davis Valley, OK 73075
(405) 238-6488
Sanctions rodeos in different
states and publishes a rodeo
news magazine.

Women's Professional Rodeo Association
Rt. 5, Box 698
Blanchard, OK 73010
(405) 485-2277
Sanctions all women's rodeos
and publishes the *Women's Pro
Rodeo News*.

OREGON

National Rooster Crowing Contest
Grants Pass Chamber
of Commerce
Grants Pass, OR 97526
(503) 476-7717
Roosters from across the nation
are entered in this contest to
see which can crow the most
times in 30 minutes; late July.

Pendleton Round-Up
Pendleton Round-Up
Association
P.O. Box 609
Pendleton, OR 97801
(800) 524-2984
(503) 276-2553
Known as the "king of rodeos,"
the event got its start in 1910
and is now one of the biggest
rodeos in North America.

World Championship Timber Carnival
Timber Carnival Association
P.O. Box 38
Albany, OR 97321
(503) 928-2391
International competition
among loggers in events such as
tree climbing, topping,
chopping, sawing, and axe
throwing; early July.

SOUTH DAKOTA

Buffalo Auction
Custer State Park
Hermosa, SD 57744
(605) 255-4515
Each year excess buffalo are put
up for auction to the visitors
who come from all over the
country; early February.

Corn Palace Festival
Mitchell Chamber
of Commerce
Mitchell, SD 57301
(605) 996-5567
Each year in September the
Corn Palace is decorated with
ears of corn; inside are exhibits
and entertainers.

Days of '76
Deadwood Chamber
of Commerce
Deadwood, SD 57732
(605) 578-1876
A wild festival including a
rodeo, gold panning, and
ceremonial dances; early
August.

Sitting Bull Stampede
Mobridge Chamber
of Commerce
Mobridge, SD 57601
(605) 845-2387
Cowboys from across the
nation participate in one of the

largest rodeos and parades;
early July.

TEXAS

Arts and Crafts Fair
Texas Arts and Crafts
Foundation
P.O. Box 1589
Kerrville, TX 78028
(512) 896-5711
Over 200 artists and
craftspeople participate.
Includes demonstrations in
soap making, blacksmithing,
and a fiddlers' contest; late May
to early June.

Black-Eyed Pea Jamboree
Athens Chamber of Commerce
P.O. Box 2600
Athens, TX 75751
(214) 675-5181
A city celebration that includes
a championship black-eyed pea
cooking contest; held for three
days in mid-July.

Breeders Cutting
National Cutting
Horse Association
P.O. Box 12155
Fort Worth, TX 76121
(817) 244-6188
A rodeo for this association
held for five days; early
October.

Charro Days
Chamber of Commerce
P.O. Box 752
Brownsville, TX 78520
(512) 542-4341
A fiesta of *charros* that straddles
two nations; March.

Chisholm Trail Round-Up
123 East Exchange Avenue
Fort Worth, TX 76106
(817) 625-7005
A mid-June city-wide
celebration of the cattle days.

Dogie Days
Chamber of Commerce
P.O. Box 735
Dumas, TX 79029
(806) 935-2123
Originally a tribute to early
settlers, this June festival now
includes a rodeo, parade, and
carnival.

El Paso Festival
El Paso Arts Alliance
333 East Missouri Street
El Paso, TX 79901
(915) 533-1700
Celebrating more than 400
years of Spanish, Indian, and
cowboy culture at El Paso del
Norte, for three days; July.

Fiesta del Concho
Convention and
Visitors Bureau
500 Rio Concho Drive
San Angelo, TX 76903
(915) 653-1206
Frontier Days celebration along
the banks of the Concho,
which includes early craft
demonstrations and the Texas
Sheep Shearing Contest; June.

Fiesta San Antonio
1145 East Commerce
San Antonio, TX 78205
(512) 227-5191
Several million people attend
this nine-day celebration, with
events including parades, a
Mexican rodeo, dancing, and
hundreds of food booths; mid-
to late April.

Heart O'Texas Fair
Chamber of Commerce
108 West Denison
Waco, TX 76706
(817) 752-6551
Held in late September, this
large fair includes traditional
livestock events, farm and
home exhibits, a rodeo, and a
midway.

Houston Livestock Show and Rodeo
P.O. Box 20070
Houston, TX 77225
(713) 791-9000
All the usual rodeo events are
found here in this major show,
held for two weeks; late
February to early March.

National Cowboy Symposium and Celebration
Division of Continuing
Education
Box 4110, TTU
Lubbock, TX 79409
(806) 742-2498
From roping and cutting to
poetry reading and scholarly
lectures, this annual event in

June studies and celebrates the
American cowboy.

National Cow-Calling Contest and Pioneer Round-Up
Chamber of Commerce
Box 66
Miami, TX 79059
(806) 868-4791
This cow-calling contest
attracts national attention; late
May to early June.

National Cowgirl Hall of Fame Rodeo
P.O. Box 1414
Hereford, TX 79045
(806) 364-5940
A cowgirls' rodeo that has all
the competitive events from
which women are usually
barred; in August.

Republic of Texas Chilympiad
P.O. Box 188
San Marcos, TX 78667
(512) 396-5400
This food festival pits one chili
lover against another for three
days; mid-September.

A San Antonio Christmas
San Antonio Convention
and Visitors Bureau
P.O. Box 2277
San Antonio, TX 78298
(512) 270-8700
A lively month-long
celebration with tours, an art
fair, Fiesta de las Luminarias,
and traditional pageants.

Tejano Conjunto Festival
1300 Guadalupe
San Antonio, TX 78207
(512) 271-3151
A festival in celebration of
Chicano music and culture;
mid-May.

Texas Cowboy Reunion
Chamber of Commerce
Box 1206
Stamford, TX 79553
(915) 773-2411
An Old West celebration and
reunion; early July.

Texas Folklife Festival
University of Texas Institute
P.O. Box 1226
San Antonio, TX 78294
(512) 226-7651
Annually in August Texans
celebrate their diverse ethnic
backgrounds through art and
celebration, exhibits and
demonstrations.

West of the Pecos Rodeo
Pecos Chamber of Commerce
Box 1127
Pecos, TX 79772
(915) 445-2406
This early-July rodeo includes
among other things a wild mare

race and wild cow milking.

World's Championship Chili Cook-Off
Texas Tourist
Development Agency
Box 12008 Capitol Station
Austin, TX 78711
(512) 320-9640
Up to 5,000 contestants,
hecklers, and spectators
converge on downtown
Terlingua for this unpredictable
event; early November.

World's Largest Rattlesnake Round-Up
P.O. Box 416
Sweetwater, TX 79556
(915) 235-5488
(915) 235-8938
Originated to help local
ranchers and farmers, this mid-
March event has gradually
taken on a life of its own.

XIT Rodeo and Reunion
Chamber of Commerce
Box 967
Dalhart, TX 79022
(806) 249-5646
Once one of the world's largest
ranches, the XIT was a
kingdom unto itself, now in
August old hands and local
residents converge for an
annual community celebration
and rodeo; August.

UTAH

Great West Fair
Festival of the American West
Old Main Building
Utah State University
116, UMC 14
Logan, UT 84322
(801) 750-1143
An opportunity in late July to
early August to see top
craftsmen of the Rocky
Mountain region.

WYOMING

Cheyenne Frontier Days
P.O. Box 2477
Cheyenne, WY 82003
(800) 543-2339
(800) 227-6336
A large outdoor rodeo with big
purses for the winners. Musical
events; last week in July.

Green River Rendezvous
Sublette County
Historical Society
P.O. Box 666
Pinedale, WY 82941
(307) 367-4367
Local folks play the part of
trappers, wagon drivers, and
other historical characters for
this rendezvous in July.

INDEX

(Page references in italics refer to photographs)

PHOTOGRAPH CREDITS